Bread Class Recipes

by Don Dickey

Over 100 High-Speed Recipes
Optimized for Classroom Use
in Adult & Continuing Education
and Programs Where Time is Limited
Developed by a Baking Instructor
with 35 Years Experience

*Textbook for Breadmaking
Beginner to Advanced*

Published by Instafax
23 Brownleigh Road
West Hartford, CT 06117
www.instafax.com

Printed in the United States of America

© 2018 by Donald K. Dickey
All rights reserved.

No part of this book may be reproduced without written permission
from the publisher, except by a reviewer who may quote brief passages
or reproduce illustrations in a review with appropriate credits, nor may any
part of this book be stored in a retrieval system or transmitted in any
form or by any means without written permission from the publisher.

The information in this book, including recommendations, is made
without guarantee on the part of the author or publisher.
The author and publisher disclaim any liability
in connection with the use of this information.

This book is available in a Instructor Kit which includes a
PDF with a site license to print recipes for classroom use.
This book is also available for special and/or promotional uses
and in customized editions, both printed and electronic.
For more information, please contact the publisher.

ISBN 978-1477457191

v3.14

This book is dedicated to
Joyce and Carolyn
who test the bread with enthusiasm
and to my students
who make this venture worthwhile.

The author also wishes to acknowledge the following
for their help and support:
West Hartford Continuing Education
Michael Jubinsky
MaryAnn Fitch
Sally Sanford
Rick Barrow

Connect with the author on
www.AtTheStove.com
for new recipes and updates
(often free of charge)
as they become available.

ABOUT THIS BOOK

There are many bread books on the market. So, what's different about this one?

Time is of the Essence
The recipes in this book are highly optimized for speed. With good organizational skills and ingredients and equipment set out by the instructor in advance, students should be able to complete most recipes within two and a half hours from start to finish.

Classroom-Tested
These recipes, particularly ones in the beginner section, can be made by inexperienced bakers including students with no previous experience with yeast-risen products.

Designed for Teaching
These recipes use common language and techniques throughout so students enjoy consistency as they progress through the book. Furthermore, recipes are typically double-size so students working in pairs each produce a loaf of bread or batch of rolls to take home. Students working in 2-person teams improves classroom efficiency since one can be mixing while the other is gathering ingredients. It is also more economical as equipment like bowls and stand mixers are shared.

Modern Ingredients & Techniques
Many bread recipes found elsewhere, including those on the internet, still use active dry yeast and include the required rehydration and proofing steps. Some even call for live cake yeast which is now almost impossible to find in markets due to its limited shelf life. This can be confusing and cause delays in the classroom as students try to convert recipes for different yeast types. This book uses only modern instant yeast, and all recipes are specially designed to take advantage of its unique properties including quick dissolving, rapid rising, and extreme reliability.

Scale Ready
Advanced students weigh ingredients instead of measuring by volume with cups and spoons. This offers several advantages: it eliminates errors from packing ingredients too tightly, it is easy to tare the scale to zero after each ingredient is added, and you end up with fewer utensils to wash when you are done. This book includes both volumes in common U.S. units and weights in grams.

Challenges for Advanced Students
Once the beginner and easy sweet dough recipes have been mastered, there are new challenges provided by whole grain baking, rustic Italian breads with high levels of hydration, and even sourdough, from capturing live yeast on local produce through to naturally risen breads.

Curriculum Driven
The author has successfully used the recipes contained in this text to teach a wide range of baking classes, including:

- *Introduction to Yeast Baking*
- *Fun with Sweet Dough*
- *Working with Whole Wheat*
- *Finger Breads (bagels, rolls, etc)*
- *Getting Started with Sourdough*
- *Bread Favorites (chosen by students)*
- *Advanced Breadmaking Topics*
- *Quick and Easy Breads*
- *A Few Famous Breads*
- *Baking by Weight*
- *Holiday Breads*
- *International Breads*
- *Rustic Italian Breads*
- *Whole Grain Breads*
- *Worldly Flatbreads*
- *Breads and Soups*
- *Breads of Brooklyn*
- *Breads of France*
- *Breads of Italy*
- *Breads of the UK*

TABLE OF CONTENTS

Introduction:
- About This Book — 4
- Basic Equipment — 6
- Primary Ingredients — 7
- Essential Techniques — 8

Recipes for Beginners:
- Basic White Bread — 9
- Universal White Dough — 10
- Bread Sticks — 11
- Classic Sandwich Bread — 12
- Easy Potato Bread — 13
- Cinnamon Swirl Bread — 14

Sweet Dough Recipes:
- Traditional Sweet Dough — 15
- Simple Sweet Dough — 16
- Filled Mock Braid — 17
- Poppy Twist — 18
- Honey Cinnamon Rolls — 19
- Nutty Sticky Buns — 20
- Swedish Tea Ring — 21
- Hot Cross Buns — 22

Finger Breads:
- Knotted Dinner Rolls — 23
- Parker House Rolls — 24
- Hawaiian Style Sweet Rolls — 25
- Onion Rye Dinner Rolls — 26
- Soft Pretzels — 27
- Bagels — 28
- Light Rye Bagels — 29
- Pumped-Up Bagels — 30
- Cranberry Orange Scones — 31
- Lemon Cream Blueberry Scones — 32
- Chocolate Chip Scones — 32
- Cranberry Orange Muffins — 33
- Apple Cinnamon Chip Muffins — 33
- Baking Powder Biscuits — 34
- Simple Drop Biscuits — 34
- Sweet Dessert Biscuits — 34

Batter Breads:
- Simple Soda Bread — 35
- Beer Bread — 35
- Corn Bread — 36
- Banana Bread — 37
- Date Nut Bread — 38
- Boston Brown Bread — 39
- Whole Wheat Batter Bread — 40

Whole Grain Breads:
- White Whole Wheat Bread — 41
- Cinnamon Swirl Wheat Bread — 42
- Golden Flax Bread — 43
- Traditional Oatmeal Bread — 44
- Quick & Easy Oatmeal Bread — 45
- Canadian Style Brown Bread — 46
- Light Rye Bread — 47
- Pumpernickel — 48
- Multigrain Bread — 49

Sourdough:
- Sourdough Culture — 50
- Pain Au Levain ~ Sourdough — 51
- Sourdough Flavored Bread — 52
- Jewish Style Rye — 53

International Breads:
- Paposecos - Portuguese Rolls — 54
- Portuguese Sweet Bread — 55
- Spanish Bread — 56
- Ensaïmadas - Mallorcan Sweet Rolls — 57
- Provencal Fougasse - French Flatbread — 58
- Pain de Campagne - Traditional Boule — 59
- Dimpled Rolls - French & Belgian Style — 60
- Petit Pains au Lait - French Milk Rolls — 61
- Pain d'Epi - French Wheat Stalk — 62
- Baguettes - Classic French Loaves — 63
- Crumpets - English Muffins — 64
- English Dinner Rolls — 65
- Cheese and Onion Bread — 66
- Saffron Cake - Cornish Recipe — 67
- Chelsea Buns — 68
- Lardy Cake - Southern Recipe — 69
- Malted Currant Bread — 70
- Spotted Dog - Irish Soda Bread — 71
- Scottish Morning Rolls — 72
- Currant Scones - Scottish Quick Breads — 73
- Bauernbrot - German Farmer's Bread — 74
- Stollen - German Christmas Bread — 75
- Babka - Authentic Polish Recipe — 76
- Bialys - Polish Bialystok Kuchen — 77
- Multigrain Polarbrød - Swedish Mjukkaka — 78
- Pulla - Finnish Cardamom Braid — 79
- Limpa - Swedish Orange Rye — 80
- Vort Limpa - Swedish Beer Bread — 81
- Russian Style Potato Bread — 82
- Black Bread - Russian Pumpernickel — 83
- Buchty - Slovakian Breakfast Treats — 84
- Kolache - Czech Filled Pastries — 85
- Ricotta Olive Bolso — 86
- Züpfe - Swiss Braid — 87
- Paratha - Leavened Indian Flatbread — 88
- Naan - Leavened Indian Flatbread — 89
- Pita - Turkish Pockets — 90
- Tortillas - Mexican Flatbreads — 91
- Balep Korkun - Tibetan Skillet Bread — 92
- Manakish Lebanese Flat Bread — 93
- Zaatar Spice Blend — 93
- Challah - Traditional Jewish Braid — 94-95
- Italian Easter Braid — 96
- Panettone - Italian Holiday Bread — 97
- Basic Dough for Italian Bread & Pizza — 98
- Stromboli — 99
- Calzones — 99

Rustic Italian Breads
- Rustic Italian no-knead Boule — 100-101
- Focaccia — 102
- Rosemary & Olive Oil Bread — 103
- Pane Rustico — 104
- Filoncino Integrale — 105
- Semolina Bread — 106
- Ciabatta — 107
- Roasted Garlic Bread — 108
- Kalamata Olive Bread — 109
- Sicilian Scroll — 110
- Pane Carasau - Sardinian Flatbread — 111

Appendix:
- Bread FAQs — 112-113
- Tips for Saving Time — 114
- Artisan Bread Tips — 115-117
- Primer on Preferments — 118-119
- Dough Scoring Designs — 120-121
- Weights of Baking Ingredients — 122-123
- Temperature Conversions — 124
- About the Author — back cover

BASIC EQUIPMENT

You don't need a lot of equipment to get started, but a few things are essential:

Large Mixing Bowl
You will need a bowl to mix batters and doughs in. A ceramic bowl's weight helps keep it from sliding around, and its thermal properties help prevent cold drafts from affecting the dough. The top should be as large as possible and still be covered by a single piece of standard plastic wrap; this translates into a 10-inch diameter bowl with a 3½-quart capacity.

Mixing Spoon
While the basic wooden spoon has been the traditional tool of choice for decades, a "spoonula" offers several advantages. It serves the function of mixing spoon and bowl-cleaning spatula at the same time, is almost impossible to break, and is easy to clean and dishwasher-safe.

Plastic Wrap
Chances are good that your grandmother draped a damp towel over rising bread. We, however, often use chemicals or a treated dryer sheet to make laundry fluffy and static-free. Do you want these chemicals in your bread? Of course not. Your grandmother didn't have plastic wrap, but we do and can take advantage of its ability to keep moisture in and bugs out.

Bench Scraper
A good bench scraper can be a tremendous help, particularly when working with extremely wet doughs common in rustic Italian breads. It can also be very useful for scraping the gluten residue off your kitchen counter. Ideally, you should have two: one metal and one plastic.

Rising Bucket
It is obviously possible to rise dough in the same bowl it is mixed in. You may prefer, however, to rise in a polyethylene canister. You can easily see through it how far the dough has risen. Furthermore, dough releases more easily from its slippery sides when it is time to turn out.

Measuring Equipment
You should have a 2-cup liquid measure, a measuring cup set for dry ingredients, and a measuring spoon set including a tablespoon (TBS) and teaspoon (tsp) at a minimum. Many bakers eventually graduate to a digital kitchen scale, but you can certainly get by without one.

Bakeware
Start with the basics: 2 loaf pans, 2 baking sheets, 2 metal cooling racks. You can add round and square baking pans later for specific recipes. Look for non-stick heavy-gage metal pans.

Bread Knife
You will certainly need a sharp, serrated bread knife. Look for one with a blade at least 9-inches long. German steel is generally regarded as the best and should stay sharp longer.

Thermometer
Most recipes in this book have recommended temperatures for liquid ingredients. A quick-read thermometer would be very useful if you want to rise as fast as possible without killing yeast.

PRIMARY INGREDIENTS

Before you begin to use these recipes, a few general instructions and tips are in order!

All-Purpose Flour
Unbleached flours are generally preferred for bread making where there is no need for the whiter color produced by bleaching. It is also possible that bleaching can weaken flour making it less appropriate for breads. For yeast-risen products, choose a sturdy flour made from hard wheat with 10~12% protein. Brands that meet this standard include Ceresota, Gold Medal Unbleached, Heckers, King Arthur, Pillsbury Unbleached, Robin Hood Unbleached, Trader Joe's "Baker Joe" brand, and Whole Foods "365" brand. Other lower-gluten flours are fine, however, for biscuits, cakes, muffins, pancakes, non-yeasted quick breads, scones, and waffles where a high level of gluten might add unwanted toughness.

Bread Flour
For certain recipes, bread flour is specified. This is because the recipe would benefit from a flour with a higher protein content. Examples would be bagels and recipes which also include flours with little or no gluten such as corn, oats, or rye. To be useful, bread flour should have at least 12% protein. Examples include Pillsbury Bread Flour, Gold Medal Better for Bread Flour, and Robin Hood Best for Bread Flour. One product that handily exceeds the standard is King Arthur Bread Flour (blue bag) at 12.7% protein.

Yeast
All recipes use instant yeast. Quick-Rise™, RapidRise™ or bread machine yeast may be substituted with similar results. These powdered products dissolve faster than granular active dry yeast and do not require rehydration prior to mixing with other ingredients. If you choose to use active dry yeast, you should rehydrate it in a quarter cup of the water or milk used in the recipe. In other words, do not add an additional quarter cup, but subtract that quarter cup used to rehydrate the yeast from the amount added later in the recipe. Allow active dry yeast to dissolve fully before adding to other ingredients. Yeast is generally added at a rate of 1½ ~2% of the weight of flour in a recipe, about 5~7 g/loaf.

Salt
All recipes in this book are based exclusively on Diamond Crystal Kosher Salt. This salt is often preferred by chefs for a number of reasons: it has no free-flowing agents, does not contain iodine (which can taste harsh), dissolves quickly, and does not bounce as much when sprinkled onto the surface of breads and other foods. You can use other salts, but a conversion factor must be applied.

> to use standard table salt - cut the quantity in half (use 50% less)
> to use Morton kosher salt - cut the quantity by a quarter (use 25% less)
> to use any other salt - use 1½~2% of the weight of flour in the recipe (about 5~7 g/loaf)

Water
With the exception of sourdough, tap water should be fine unless it smells of chlorine. Always use de-chlorinated water for starter-leavened sourdough since its natural yeast is very sensitive.

Additives
These recipes do not include additives such as barley malt (yeast food) or ascorbic acid (dough conditioner). While such additives may improve performance in some situations, a good recipe made with good ingredients should not need additives. For recipes with 25% or more non-wheat flour (e.g. corn, oats, or rye) you could, however, boost the protein by adding 1~2 TBS of vital wheat gluten. As mentioned above, such recipes typically also call for the use of high-gluten bread flour.

ESSENTIAL TECHNIQUES

Always read through the entire recipe and assemble all ingredients before beginning!

Flour Measurement
Flour should be measured by the "spoon and sweep" method: lightly spoon the flour into the measuring cup and then sweep off the excess with a spatula. Scooping flour with the measuring cup (referred to as "scoop & sweep") can pack in as much as 25% additional flour and will result in inaccurate measurements. Note that flour quantities listed in recipes are approximate. Several factors can affect how much flour will be needed on a given day including humidity and the types of flours used.

Scalding Milk
Some recipes call for scalding milk. This is to deactivate a protein in milk, specifically in the whey, which can slightly reduce the volume of yeast-risen bread. Regular non-fat instant dry milk also contains this protein and may similarly be rehydrated and scalded for maximum volume. To scald milk, heat it nearly to a boil, 180°F (82°C), or more. You might see a skin form on the surface just before the milk boils. Take it off-heat and discard any skin that formed on top. In any event, avoid scorching the milk by heating it too much. To skip scalding and maintain maximum bread volume, you can use ultra-high temperature (labeled "UHT") dry milk or shelf-stable liquid milk such as Parmalat.

Rising
You can speed up rising cycles using the oven as a "proofing chamber" by warming it slightly to 100°F and turning it off. Understand that dough develops flavor and character while it rises, and hastening the rise can have a detrimental effect on the final product. This is why artisan bakers often retard the rise.

Punching Down
Many old bread recipes call for punching dough down to degas it. This can also break up the gluten strands you've worked hard to develop. Instead, many of the recipes in this book instruct you to fold the dough on itself several times (like a business letter) followed by briefly kneading it. This is sometimes referred to as "taking a turn on the dough." Treat risen artisan doughs gently for best results.

Pan Preparation
Cornmeal is often used to help prevent dough from sticking to pans, but its use should be limited to recipes which bake at 375°F or less. At higher temperatures, cornmeal can burn and give your products an off-taste. For high-temp baking, use either plain flour or semolina, a coarse wheat flour typically used to make pasta. You can use a light spray of release (PAM) to encourage cornmeal or semolina to stick to the sides of a baking pan. Parchment paper is also useful as a pan liner with or without semolina.

Nomenclature
TBS = tablespoon
tsp = teaspoon
C = cup
# = pound

Conversions
1 TBS = 3 tsp = 15 ml
1 C = 8 ounces = 16 TBS = 237 ml
1 Quart = 4 C = 32 ounces = 946 ml
1 Liter = 34 ounces
1 # = 16 ounces = 454 grams
1 Kg = 2.2 # = 35 ounces

BASIC WHITE BREAD

2 C	472 g	Warm Water (120°~130°F)
5⅓ C	640 g	All-Purpose Flour (approx)
1 TBS	10 g	Instant Yeast
1 TBS	10 g	Salt (DC kosher)
1 TBS	11 g	Semolina for dusting pan

> **Recipe Tip**
> Lean breads with no fat stale quickly, so enjoy them soon.

- Measure warm water into a large mixing bowl.
- Mix in 3 C of flour; stir briskly until smooth.
- With batter temperature under 110°F, mix in yeast.
- Optionally, let batter rest 15~30 minutes (autolyse) while sponge develops.
- Mix in salt and then 2 C of flour, one at a time.
- Mix in additional flour, ¼ C at a time, until dough starts to release from bowl.
- Dust dough and counter lightly with flour and turn dough out.
- Knead until dough is smooth and elastic, adding flour only as necessary.
- Rise, covered, in a lightly oiled bowl until doubled in bulk.
- Prepare sheet pan with parchment (optional); sprinkle pan with semolina.
- Fold risen dough on itself a few times; knead briefly; divide in half.
- Shape dough into loaves and place on prepared pan.
- Bake per instructions below; cool on a wire rack before cutting or storing.

Quick Method:
- Let loaves rise for 15 minutes in a cold oven.
- Slash tops diagonally with serrated knife.
- Turn oven temperature to 375°F and bake 35~40 minutes until done.

Standard Method:
- Rise loaves, covered, until almost doubled.
- Preheat oven to 375°F while loaves rises.
- Slash tops diagonally with serrated knife.
- Bake in preheated oven 30~35 minutes until done.

UNIVERSAL WHITE DOUGH
for loaves or rolls

1¾ C	413 g	Warm Water (120°~130°F)
¼ C	17 g	Instant Dry Milk (optional)
1 TBS	13 g	Granulated Sugar
5½ C	660 g	All-Purpose Flour (approx)
1 TBS	10 g	Instant Yeast
1 TBS	9 g	Salt (DC kosher)
¼ C	55 g	Vegetable Oil
1 TBS	11 g	Semolina for dusting pan

- Measure warm water into a large mixing bowl.
- Mix in milk, sugar, and 2½ C of flour; stir briskly until smooth.
- With batter temperature under 110°F, mix in yeast.
- Optionally, let batter rest 15~30 minutes (autolyse) while sponge develops.
- Mix in salt, oil, and then 2½ C of flour, one C at a time.
- Mix in additional flour, ¼ C at a time, until dough starts to release from bowl.
- Dust dough and counter lightly with flour and turn dough out.
- Knead until dough is smooth and elastic, adding flour only as necessary.
- Rise, covered, in a lightly oiled bowl until doubled in bulk.

for loaves

- Prepare sheet pan with parchment (optional); sprinkle pan with semolina.
- Fold dough on itself a few times; knead briefly; divide in half.
- Shape dough into loaves and place on prepared baking pan.
- Rise, covered, until almost doubled. Do not allow to over-rise.
- Preheat oven to 375°F while dough rises.
- Slash tops with serrated knife and bake 30~35 minutes until done.
- Remove from pans; cool on a wire rack before cutting or storing.

for rolls

- Lightly butter the sides of two 8-inch square cake pans.
- Line the bottoms of the pans with parchment cut to fit.
- Fold dough on itself a few times; knead briefly; divide in half.
- Divide each half into 9 or 16 round pieces (for large or small rolls).
- Coat each piece with melted butter and place into prepared pans.
- Allow dough to rise, covered, until almost but not quite doubled.
- Preheat oven to 375°F while dough rises.
- Bake 20~25 minutes until golden and just done; do not over-bake.
- Enjoy warm or cool on a wire rack before storing.

BREAD STICKS

1½ C	354 g	Warm Water (120°~130°F)
2 TBS	25 g	Sugar
4¾ C	570 g	All-Purpose Flour (approx)
1 TBS	9 g	Instant Yeast
1 TBS	9 g	Salt (DC kosher)
4 TBS	57 g	Butter, softened (½ stick)
2 TBS	21 g	Semolina for dusting pans
½ tsp	3 g	Garlic Salt (optional)

BEGINNERS

- Measure warm water into a large mixing bowl.
- Mix in sugar and 2 C of flour; stir briskly until smooth.
- With batter temperature under 110°F, mix in yeast.
- Optionally, let batter rest 15~30 minutes (autolyse) while sponge develops.
- Mix in salt and butter; mix in 2 C of flour, one at a time.
- Mix in additional flour, ¼ C at a time, until dough starts to release from bowl.
- Dust dough and counter lightly with flour and turn dough out.
- Knead until dough is smooth and elastic, adding flour only as necessary.
- Shape dough into a tight ball.
- Rise, covered, in a lightly oiled bowl until doubled in bulk.
- Fold dough on itself a few times and knead briefly.
- Preheat oven to 400°F while you continue with the recipe.
- Prepare sheet pan with parchment (optional); sprinkle pan with semolina.
- Using bench scraper, divide dough into 16 equal pieces.
- Roll each piece into a ½-inch diameter rope and place on prepared pan.
- Space ropes about ½-inch apart so they won't rise into each other.
- Spray ropes lightly with oil (PAM).
- Rise, covered, until almost but not quite doubled.
- Bake 15~18 minutes until golden and just done; do not over-bake.
- Optionally, brush with melted butter and sprinkle with garlic salt.
- Enjoy warm or cool on a wire rack before storing.

Recipe Tips
Add roasted garlic to the dough for added flavor without the bite of regular garlic. Try roasted garlic slices pulverized with mortar and pestle or purchase granulated roasted garlic from your favorite purveyor.

CLASSIC SANDWICH BREAD

2 C	472 g	Warm Water (120°~130°F)
⅓ C	23 g	Instant Dry Milk
¼ C	50 g	Sugar (or Honey)
5¾ C	690 g	All-Purpose Flour (approx)
1 TBS	10 g	Instant Yeast
¼ C	55 g	Oil (or melted butter/margarine)
1 TBS	10 g	Salt (DC kosher)
1 TBS	11 g	Semolina for dusting pans

- Measure warm water into a large mixing bowl.
- Mix in milk, sugar, and 3 C of flour; stir briskly until smooth.
- With batter temperature under 110°F, mix in yeast.
- Optionally, let batter rest 15~30 minutes (autolyse) while sponge develops.
- Mix in oil and salt; mix in 2 C of flour, one at a time.
- Mix in additional flour, ¼ C at a time, until dough starts to release from bowl.
- Dust dough and counter lightly with flour and turn dough out.
- Knead until dough is smooth and elastic, adding flour only as necessary.
- Rise, covered, in a lightly oiled bowl until doubled in bulk.
- Lightly spray two loaf pans with release (PAM) and sprinkle with semolina.
- Fold dough on itself a few times; knead briefly; divide in half.
- Shape into loaves and place in prepared baking pans.
- Rise, covered, until almost doubled.
- Preheat oven to 375°F while dough rises.
- Lightly dust tops of loaves with flour; slash tops with one long stroke.
- Bake 30~35 minutes until done.
- Remove from pans; cool on a wire rack before cutting or storing.

> **Recipe Tip**
> A loaf pan is recommended for two reasons: slices will be perfect for sandwiches, and the pan supports the dough as it rises.

EASY POTATO BREAD

2 C	472 g	Warm Water (120°~130°F)
½ C	33 g	Instant Potato Flakes
¼ C	17 g	Instant Dry Milk
2 TBS	25 g	Sugar (or Honey)
5 C	600 g	Bread Flour (approx)
1 TBS	11 g	Instant Yeast
¼ C	55 g	Oil or Softened Butter
1 large	50 g	Egg, beaten (optional)
1 TBS	11 g	Salt (DC kosher)
1 TBS	11 g	Semolina for dusting pans

BEGINNERS

- Mix potato flakes into warm water in a large mixing bowl.
- Mix in milk, sugar and 1 C of flour; stir briskly until smooth.
- With batter temperature under 110°F, mix in yeast.
- Optionally, let batter rest 15~30 minutes (autolyse) while sponge develops.
- Mix in oil, egg, and salt; mix in 3 C of flour, one at a time.
- Mix in additional flour, ¼ C at a time, until dough starts to release from bowl.
- Dust dough and counter lightly with flour and turn dough out.
- Knead until dough is smooth and elastic, adding flour only as necessary.
- Rise, covered, in a lightly oiled bowl until doubled in bulk.
- Lightly spray two loaf pans with release (PAM) and sprinkle with semolina.
- Fold dough on itself a few times; knead briefly; divide in half.
- Shape into loaves and place in prepared baking pans.
- Rise, covered, until almost doubled.
- Preheat oven to 375°F while dough rises.
- Lightly dust tops of loaves with flour; slash tops with a sharp knife.
- Bake 35~40 minutes until done.
- Remove from pans; cool on a wire rack before cutting or storing.

Recipe Tips

- This bread is excellent toasted. Its open crumb is perfect for butter or jam.

- For real potatoes instead of flakes, use 1 C of mashed and 1¼ C of milk; mix and warm to 110°F and continue with step 2.

CINNAMON SWIRL BREAD

1½ C	354 g	Hot Water (180°F)
1 C	160 g	Raisins (optional)
½ C	35 g	Instant Dry Milk
¼ C	50 g	Granulated Sugar
¼ C	55 g	Brown Sugar
¼ C	56 g	Butter, softened
1 large	19 g	Egg yolk (reserve white)
1 large	50 g	Egg (whole), beaten
1 TBS	10 g	Instant Yeast
1 TBS	10 g	Salt (DC kosher)
5½ C	660 g	All-Purpose Flour (approx)
1 large	30 g	Egg white (reserved)
2 TBS	42 g	Honey (as required)
2 TBS	10 g	Cinnamon (as required)

- Measure hot water into a large mixing bowl.
- Plump raisins, if desired, in the hot water ~ 3 minutes.
- While raisins plump, separate one egg and set white aside.
- Beat yolk and whole egg together in a small bowl.
- Mix milk, sugars, butter and beaten eggs with water/raisins.
- Beat in 2 C flour, one cup at a time to make a batter.
- Check batter temperature; when under 110°F mix in yeast.
- Optionally, let batter rest 15~30 minutes (autolyse) while sponge develops.
- Mix in salt and 3 C of flour, one cup at a time.
- Mix in additional flour, ¼ C at a time, until dough just releases from bowl.
- Dust dough and counter lightly with flour and turn dough out.
- Knead until dough is smooth and elastic, adding flour only as necessary.
- Rise, covered, in a lightly oiled bowl until doubled in bulk.
- Fold dough on itself a few times; knead briefly; divide in half.
- Cover and rest 5~10 minutes.
- While dough rests, mix 2 TBS honey into 2 TBS reserved egg white.
- Line bottoms of two 8½ x 4½-inch loaf pans with parchment; butter sides.
- Roll out each half to a rectangle 7 inches wide x 16 inches deep.
- Spread with thin layer of honey mix, leaving a half-inch border around outside.
- Sprinkle heavily with cinnamon.
- Roll up from far short edge towards you; pinch seams and ends to seal.
- Place loaves in prepared pans with seam side down.
- Rise, covered, until almost but not quite doubled.
- Preheat oven to 375°F while dough rises.
- Bake 30~35 minutes until done.
- Remove from pans; cool on a wire rack before cutting or storing.

TRADITIONAL SWEET DOUGH

1½ C	366 g	Milk, scalded
1/2 C	113 g	Butter/Margarine (1 stick)
1/2 C	100 g	Sugar
2 tsp	8 g	Vanilla Extract (optional)
2 large	100 g	Eggs, beaten
4 tsp	12 g	Instant Yeast
4 tsp	12 g	Salt (DC kosher)
6¾ C	810 g	All-Purpose Flour (approx)

- Warm eggs in hot tap water while you continue.
- Scald milk in saucepan or microwave to 180°F.
- Add butter/margarine to hot milk; stir and allow to melt.
- Dissolve sugar in warm milk mixture; add vanilla if desired.
- In a large bowl, beat eggs.
- Add milk mixture to eggs.
- Mix in 3 C of flour, one at a time; beat well.
- With batter temperature under 110°F, mix in yeast.
- Optionally, let batter rest 15~30 minutes (autolyse) while sponge develops.
- Mix in salt.
- Mix in 3 C of flour, one at a time.
- Mix in additional flour, ¼ C at a time, until dough starts to release from bowl.
- Dust dough and counter lightly with flour and turn dough out.
- Knead until dough is smooth and elastic, adding flour only as necessary.
- Rise, covered, in a lightly oiled bowl until doubled in bulk.
- Fold dough on itself a few times; knead briefly; divide in half.
- After an optional 10~15 minute rest (covered) shape as required.

Recipe Tips

- No time to scald? Use shelf stable ultra high temperature (UHT) milk available at most supermarkets. You can keep some in your pantry for baking or other emergencies as it does not require refrigeration until opened.

SIMPLE SWEET DOUGH

1½ C	354 g	Warm Water (120°~130°F)
½ C	35 g	Instant Dry Milk
½ C	100 g	Sugar
4 tsp	11 g	Instant Yeast
½ C	109 g	Oil (or melted butter/margarine)
2 large	100 g	Eggs, beaten
2 tsp	8 g	Vanilla Extract (optional)
4 tsp	11 g	Salt (DC kosher)
6¼ C	750 g	All-Purpose Flour (approx)

- Warm eggs in hot tap water while you continue.
- Measure warm water into a large mixing bowl.
- Mix in milk, sugar, and 2 C of flour; stir briskly until smooth.
- With batter temperature under 110°F, mix in yeast.
- Optionally, let batter rest 15~30 minutes (autolyse) while sponge develops.
- Mix in oil, beaten eggs, vanilla, and salt.
- Mix in 3 C of flour, one at a time.
- Mix in additional flour, ¼ C at a time, until dough starts to release from bowl.
- Dust dough and counter lightly with flour and turn dough out.
- Knead until dough is smooth and elastic, adding flour only as necessary.
- Rise, covered, in a lightly oiled bowl until doubled in bulk.
- Fold dough on itself a few times; knead briefly; divide in half.
- After an optional 10~15 minute rest (covered) shape as required.

> **Recipe Tip**
> - Rise dough in a polyethylene canister. You can see when it is double, and dough releases from its slippery surface easily when it is time to turn out.

FILLED MOCK BRAID

1 recipe	Sweet Dough
1 can	Cake & Pastry Filling (Almond, Poppy, Raspberry, etc)
	Egg Yolk, beaten with 1 tsp water (optional for wash)

- Make sweet dough recipe and allow to rise until doubled in bulk.
- Preheat oven to 350°F while you make and rise the braids.
- Prepare 2 sheet pans with parchment.
- Divide dough in half (sweet dough recipe makes 2 braids).
- Roll dough out to a rectangle about 10 x 18 inches.
- Place dough on cutting board.
- Spread filling down middle third of dough.
- Make equal number of 1-inch diagonal slits along both sides.
- Cut only a third of the way in on each side and not into the filling.
- Fold far end down over filling.
- Start at far end, lace up dough fingers from alternating sides.
- Fold bottom end in and seal by pinching.
- Rise, covered, on prepared sheet pan to almost but not quite double.
- For a glossy finish, brush with egg wash just before baking (optional).
- Bake 30~35 minutes until done.
- Cool on a wire rack before cutting or storing.
- When cool, dust with confectioners' sugar if desired.

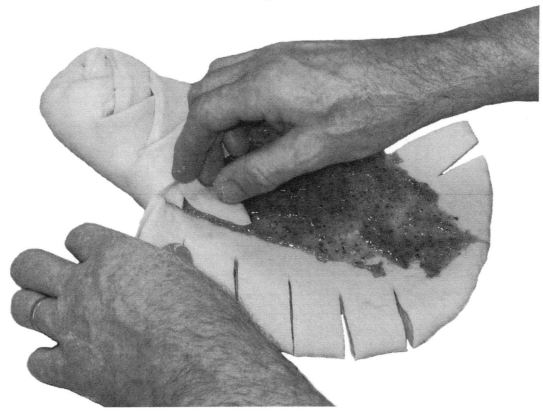

POPPY TWIST

1 recipe	Sweet Dough
1 can	Poppy Cake & Pastry Filling
	Egg Yolk, beaten with 1 tsp water (optional for wash)

- Make sweet dough recipe and allow to rise until doubled in bulk.
- Preheat oven to 350°F while you make and rise the twists.
- Prepare 2 sheet pans with parchment.
- Divide dough in half (sweet dough recipe makes 2 twists).
- Roll out dough into a 15-inch square.
- Spread filing over dough leaving a 1-inch border around filling.
- Roll up as for jelly roll; pinch to seal; turn so the seam side is down.
- Starting a couple inches in from an end cut through roll the long way using multiple strokes with a very sharp knife.
- Turn the 2 halves so the cut sides are up.
- Braid the pieces passing one side under the other keeping the cut side up.
- Rise, covered, on prepared sheet pan to almost but not quite double.
- For a glossy finish, brush with egg wash just before baking (optional).
- Bake 30-35 minutes until golden and done.
- Cool on a wire rack before cutting or storing.

based on techniques by Michael Jubinsky
photo by Tony Musano

HONEY CINNAMON ROLLS

Rolls

1 recipe		Sweet Dough
2 TBS	42 g	Honey
1 large	30 g	Egg white
2 TBS	10 g	Ground Cinnamon
1 large	19 g	Egg Yolk, beaten with 1 tsp water (optional for wash)

Glaze

¾ C	58 g	Confectioners' Sugar
¼ C	58 g	Heavy Cream
1 tsp	4 g	Vanilla Extract (clear if possible)

- Make sweet dough recipe and allow to rise until doubled in bulk.
- Preheat oven to 375°F while you make and rise the rolls.
- Prepare a sheet pan with parchment.
- Mix honey into egg white.
- Divide dough in half. Roll each piece out to 16x16 inch square.
- Brush surface with thin coating of honey mix; sprinkle heavily with cinnamon.
- Roll up toward you into a log as for a jelly roll.
- Cut log into slices ~ 1½ inches thick.
- Place rolls on prepared pan in pairs with tails touching to prevent unwinding.
- Allow rolls to rise ~20 minutes until almost but not quite double.
- For a glossy finish, brush with egg wash just before baking (optional).
- Bake 20~25 minutes until golden brown and just done; do not over-bake.
- Enjoy warm or cool on a wire rack before storing.
- Glaze cooled rolls if desired just before serving.

> **Recipe Tips**
> If you're out of honey, try this: brush dough with melted butter and sprinkle with cinnamon sugar. Use brown sugar more robust flavor.

NUTTY STICKY BUNS

1 recipe		Sweet Dough
½ C	113 g	Butter/Margarine (1 stick)
1 C	238 g	Brown Sugar
¼ C	80 g	Dark Corn Syrup
2 TBS	30 g	Water
1 C	140 g	Nuts, chopped
1 tsp	2 g	Cinnamon

- Make sweet dough recipe and allow to rise until doubled in bulk.
- Melt butter/margarine in a small saucepan.
- Stir in brown sugar and heat until dissolved.
- Pour off 2 TBS of butter/sugar mix for later.
- Add corn syrup and water to saucepan; mix.
- Pour equal amounts of sauce into two 9 inch cake pans.
- Sprinkle ¼ C of nuts in each pan.
- When dough has doubled, divide in half.
- Preheat oven to 350°F while you make and rise the buns.
- Roll each half out to 12 x 12 inches.
- Spread each half with 1 TBS of reserved butter/sugar mix.
- Dust each with some cinnamon and ¼ C of nuts.
- Roll up toward you into a log as for a jelly roll.
- Cut log into 7 equal size slices and place into prepared pans.
- Allow rolls to rise 20~30 minutes until almost but not quite double.
- Bake ~ 25 minutes until browned and just done; do not over-bake.
- Loosen edges and invert over a plate, pan included.
- When syrup has drained, remove pan.
- Enjoy warm or cool before storing.

SWEDISH TEA RING

| 1 recipe | | Sweet Dough |
| 1 can | | Almond Pastry Filling |

Glaze

¾ C	58 g	Confectioners' Sugar
¼ C	58 g	Heavy Cream
1 tsp	4 g	Vanilla Extract (clear preferred)

- Make sweet dough recipe and allow to rise until doubled in bulk.
- Preheat oven to 350°F while you make and rise the rings.
- Prepare 2 sheet pans with parchment.
- Divide dough in half (full dough recipe makes 2 rings).
- Roll dough out to a rectangle ~ 14 x 18 inches.
- Spread filling over dough leaving a half-inch border around filling (figure 1).
- Roll up toward you as for a jelly roll (figure 2).
- Pull roll into a wreath and join ends (figure 3).
- Make cuts ¾ way through dough (figure 4).
- Twist segments 45° ~ 90° (figure 5).
- Rise, covered, on parchment to almost but not quite double.
- For a glossy finish, brush with an egg wash just before baking (optional).
- Bake 30 ~ 35 minutes until done. Tent with foil if necessary to stop browning.
- Cool on a wire rack before glazing or storing.

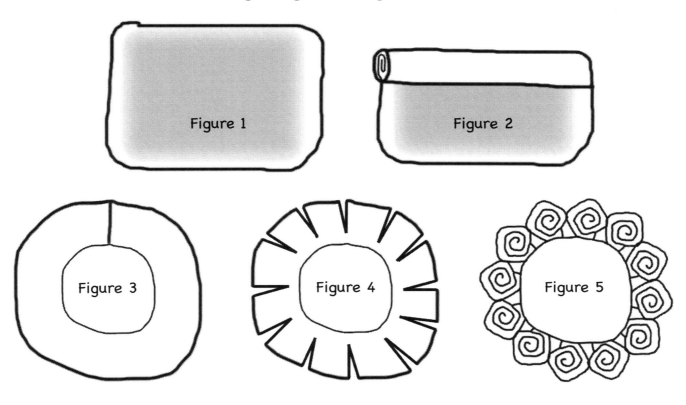

HOT CROSS BUNS

1¼ C	295 g	Hot Water or Scalded Milk
1 C	160 g	Raisins
⅓ C	23 g	Instant Dry Milk (only if using water)
⅓ C	67 g	Sugar
½ C	109 g	Oil (or melted butter/margarine)
2 large	100 g	Eggs, beaten (reserve ½ TBS for wash)
1 TBS	10 g	Instant Yeast
1 TBS	10 g	Salt (DC kosher)
2 tsp	9 g	Baking Powder
1 tsp	2 g	Spice (½ tsp Cinnamon, ¼ tsp Nutmeg, ¼ tsp Allspice)
2 tsp	9 g	Vanilla Extract
5½ C	660 g	All-Purpose Flour (approx)

- Warm eggs in hot tap water while you continue.
- Measure hot water or scalded milk into a large mixing bowl.
- Add raisins and allow to plump 2~3 minutes.
- Mix in dry milk, sugar, oil, beaten eggs, and 2 C of flour. Beat well.
- With batter temperature under 110°F, mix in yeast.
- Optionally, let batter rest 15~30 minutes (autolyse) while sponge develops.
- Mix in salt, baking powder, spice, vanilla, and 3 C of flour, one at a time.
- Mix in additional flour, ¼ C at a time, until dough starts to release from bowl.
- Dust dough and counter lightly with flour and turn dough out.
- Knead until dough is smooth and elastic, adding flour only as necessary.
- Rise, covered, in a lightly oiled bowl until doubled in bulk.
- Fold dough on itself a few times; knead briefly; allow to rest 10 minutes.
- Preheat oven to 375°F while you make and rise the buns.
- Reserve a 3-inch ball of dough, covered.
- Divide remaining dough in half.
- Shape each half into 9 equal size balls.
- Grease two 8-inch square cake pans.
- Place 9 balls into each pan (3 rows of 3 balls).
- Cut a cross in the tops of the buns.
- Make a ¼ inch diameter rope from the reserved dough.
- Place a cross made from the rope into the cuts in each bun.
- Beat the reserved egg with ½ tsp of water and brush tops.
- Allow buns to rise 20~30 minutes until almost but not quite double.
- Bake ~20 minutes until golden brown and just done; do not over-bake.
- Transfer to a wire rack to cool before storing.
- When buns are cool, ice crosses if desired with your favorite icing.

> **Recipe Tip**
> If you plan on freezing these buns, do not ice the crosses until just before serving.

based on techniques by Michael Jubinsky

KNOTTED DINNER ROLLS

1½ C	354 g	Warm Water (120°~130°F)
¼ C	17 g	Instant Dry Milk
¼ C	50 g	Sugar
6 C	720 g	All-Purpose Flour (approx)
1 TBS	11 g	Instant Yeast
1 TBS	11 g	Salt (DC kosher)
2 large	100 g	Eggs, beaten
1 large	19 g	Egg Yolk, beaten (reserve white)
2 TBS	25 g	Shortening
2 TBS	28 g	Butter (soft)
2 TBS	21 g	Semolina for dusting pans
1 large	30 g	Egg White, beaten with 1 tsp Water
1 TBS	10 g	Poppy or Sesame Seeds (optional)

SWEET DOUGH

- Warm eggs in hot tap water while you continue.
- Measure warm water into a large mixing bowl.
- Mix in milk, sugar and 2 C of flour; stir briskly until smooth.
- With batter temperature under 110°F, mix in yeast.
- Optionally, let batter rest 15~30 minutes (autolyse) while sponge develops.
- Mix in salt, 2 eggs + 1 yolk (beaten), shortening, and butter.
- Mix in 3 C of flour, one at a time.
- Mix in additional flour, ¼ C at a time, until dough starts to release from bowl.
- Dust dough and counter lightly with flour and turn dough out.
- Knead until dough is smooth and elastic, adding flour only as necessary.
- Rise, covered, in a lightly oiled bowl until doubled in bulk.
- Fold dough on itself a few times and knead briefly.
- Preheat oven to 375°F while you continue with the recipe.
- Prepare sheet pan with parchment (optional); sprinkle pan with semolina.
- Divide dough into 16 equal size pieces.
- Roll pieces into ropes about 12 inches long.
- Tie a simple overhand knot in a rope.
- Flip each end around the rope again, one over and the other under.
- Press the ends together to complete the knot.
- Place knotted roll on prepared pan.
- Repeat knotting process with other ropes.
- Rise until almost but not quite double (20~30 minutes).
- For shiny finish: brush with egg wash and sprinkle with seeds if desired OR
- For a soft finish, brush with melted butter.
- Bake 15~20 minutes until golden and just done; do not over-bake.
- Enjoy warm or cool on a wire rack before storing.

PARKER HOUSE ROLLS

2 large	38 g	Egg Yolks
1½ C	366 g	Very Warm Milk (140°F)
⅓ C	67 g	Sugar
1 TBS	10 g	Instant Yeast
2 tsp	7 g	Salt (DC kosher)
6 TBS	85 g	Butter, softened (¾ stick)
5 C	600 g	All-Purpose Flour (approx)
2 TBS	28 g	Butter, melted (for glazing)

- Warm eggs in hot tap water while you continue.
- Measure warm milk into a large bowl.
- Mix in sugar and 2 C of flour to create a batter.
- With batter temperature under 110°F, mix in yeast.
- Let batter rest for 15~30 minutes (autolyse) while sponge develops.
- Separate eggs: yolks for this recipe and whites for other recipes.
- Beat yolks; then mix yolks into batter.
- Mix salt and 6 TBS butter into batter, approximately 1 TBS at a time.
- Beat in 2 C of flour, 1 C at a time; mix until well incorporated.
- Mix in additional flour, ¼ C at a time, until dough starts to release from bowl.
- Dust dough and counter lightly with flour and turn dough out.
- Knead until dough is smooth and elastic, adding flour only as necessary.
- Shape dough into a tight ball.
- Rise, covered, in a lightly oiled bowl until doubled in bulk.
- Preheat oven to 375°F while the dough rises.
- Prepare 9x13 baking pan with parchment; spray with release (PAM).
- Fold dough on itself a few times and knead briefly.
- Divide dough in half and then divide each half into 12 pieces.
- Shape each piece into a smooth ball and place in prepared pan.
- Allow rolls to rise, covered, until not quite double, 20~30 minutes.
- Brush rolls with butter just before baking.
- Bake to golden and just done, about 15~18 minutes; do not over-bake.
- Optionally, brush with butter again just before serving.
- Enjoy warm or cool on a wire rack before storing.

Recipe Info

The original recipe was created at the Parker House Hotel in Boston during the 1870s. Supposedly an angry pastry cook threw unfinished rolls into the oven which caused their dented appearance.

photo by Tony Musano

HAWAIIAN STYLE SWEET ROLLS

12 oz	370 g	Evaporated Milk (1 can)
½ C	113 g	Butter/Margarine (1 stick)
¾ C	150 g	Sugar
1 tsp	4 g	Vanilla Extract
1 TBS	6 g	Zest of 1 Lemon
4 large	200 g	Eggs, beaten
1 TBS	10 g	Instant Yeast (SAF Gold preferred)
1 TBS	10 g	Salt (DC kosher)
6½ C	780 g	All-Purpose Flour (approx)

- Warm eggs in hot tap water while you continue.
- Heat milk in a saucepan or microwave; do not burn.
- Add butter/margarine to hot milk; stir to melt.
- Dissolve sugar in milk mixture; mix in vanilla, lemon, and beaten eggs.
- Check temperature; re-warm liquids to 120°F if necessary.
- Transfer liquids to a large (warmed) mixing bowl.
- Mix in 3 C of flour; beat well by hand or with mixer.
- With batter temperature under 110°F, mix in yeast.
- Optionally, let batter rest 15~30 minutes (autolyse) while sponge develops.
- Mix in salt and then 3 C additional flour, one cup at a time.
- Mix in up to ¼ C more flour until dough starts to release from bowl.
- Dust top of dough and counter with last ¼ C flour and turn dough out.
- Knead until dough is smooth and elastic, adding flour only as necessary.
- Rise, covered, in a lightly oiled bowl until doubled in bulk.
- Lightly grease the sides of two 9-inch round cake pans.
- Line the bottoms of the pans with parchment cut to fit.
- Fold dough on itself a few times; knead briefly; divide in half.
- Divide each half into 12 equal size pieces (~ 65g each).
- Shape dough into round balls; place into prepared pans.
- Allow dough to rise, covered, until almost but not quite doubled.
- Preheat oven to 350°F while dough rises.
- Bake 25~30 minutes until golden and done.
- Tent tops with foil if they appear to be browning too rapidly.
- Brush hot rolls with melted butter (optional); serve warm.

> **Recipe Tips**
> - Using evaporated milk makes this recipe authentic.
> - To stretch the recipe add up to ½ C water to liquids plus ~ 1¼ C additional flour making 15~18 rolls to rise and bake in a 9 x 13 inch rectangular pan.

ONION RYE DINNER ROLLS

1¼ C	305 g	Milk, scalded
4 TBS	57 g	Butter (1/2 stick)
2 TBS	42 g	Honey
½ C	118 g	Water
1 TBS	10 g	Instant Yeast
1 TBS	10 g	Salt (DC kosher)
2 TBS	18 g	Caraway Seeds
⅓ C	60 g	Onion, minced
1½ C	180 g	Rye Flour
3¼ C	390 g	Bread Flour (approx)
1 TBS	11 g	Semolina for dusting pans
Wash	optional	Egg beaten with 1 TBS Water

- Scald milk in saucepan or microwave to 180°F; do not burn.
- Add butter to hot milk; stir to melt.
- Mix in honey and water; adjust temp to 120°F as required.
- Transfer liquids to a large (warmed) mixing bowl.
- Mix in 2½ C of bread flour; stir briskly until smooth.
- With batter temperature under 110°F, mix in yeast.
- Optionally, let batter rest 15~30 minutes (autolyse) while sponge develops.
- Mix in salt, seeds (if desired), and onion.
- Mix in rye flour.
- Mix in bread flour (~ ½ C) until dough starts to release from bowl.
- Dust dough and counter with last ¼ C bread flour and turn dough out.
- Knead until dough forms a smooth ball, adding flour only as necessary.
- Rise, covered, in an oiled bowl until doubled in bulk.
- Fold dough on itself a few times; divide in half.
- Prepare sheet pan with parchment (optional); sprinkle pan with semolina.
- Roll dough into ropes; cut each rope into 12 equal size pieces.
- Shape dough into smooth round balls; place onto prepared pans.
- Allow dough to rise, covered, until almost but not quite doubled.
- Preheat oven to 400°F while dough rises.
- Optionally, brush rolls with egg wash just before baking.
- Bake 18~20 minutes until nicely browned and done.
- Transfer to a wire rack; serve warm.

> **Recipe Tip**
> Caraway seeds aren't for everyone!
> If you don't like them, leave them out.

SOFT PRETZELS

1½ C	354 g	Warm Water (120°~130°F)
1 TBS	13 g	Sugar
1 TBS	9 g	Instant Yeast
2 tsp	6 g	Salt (DC kosher)
4 TBS	57 g	Butter, softened (½ stick)
5 C	600 g	All-Purpose Flour (approx)
9 C	2 L	Water
½ C	111 g	Baking Soda
2 TBS	28 g	Oil or spray (PAM) for pans
1 large	19 g	Egg Yolk for wash
1 TBS	15 g	Water for wash
1 tsp	5 g	Coarse Salt for topping

- Measure warm water into a large mixing bowl.
- Mix in sugar and 2 C of flour; stir briskly until smooth.
- With batter temperature under 110°F, mix in yeast.
- Optionally, let batter rest 15~30 minutes (autolyse) while sponge develops.
- Mix in kosher salt and butter; mix in 2½ C of flour, half at a time.
- Mix in additional flour, ¼ C at a time, until dough starts to release from bowl.
- Dust dough and counter lightly with flour and turn dough out.
- Knead until dough is smooth and elastic, adding flour only as necessary.
- Shape dough into a tight ball.
- Rise, covered, in a lightly oiled bowl until doubled in bulk.
- Prepare 2 sheet pans with parchment; brush with oil (or spray with PAM).
- Boil water in a wide pot; mix in baking soda; also preheat oven to 450°F.
- Beat egg yolk with 1 TBS water to make a wash.
- Fold doubled dough on itself a few times; knead briefly; divide in half.
- Divide one half of dough into 4 equal (~125 g) pieces.
- Roll one piece of dough into a 24-inch long rope.
- Form the rope into a U with the legs ~3 inches apart.
- Cross the ends of the dough and press onto the bottom of the U.
- Place shaped pretzels onto the prepared pan.
- Repeat the shaping process with the remaining 3 pieces of dough.
- Boil each pretzel (one at a time) for 30 seconds.
- Drain on spatula or skimmer; return drained pretzels to prepared pan.
- Brush pretzels with egg wash.
- Sprinkle with coarse salt or other toppings as desired.
- Bake 12~14 minutes until golden brown and done.
- While first 4 pretzels bake, shape and boil the second batch.
- Transfer baked pretzels to a wire rack; cool briefly; enjoy warm.

BAGELS

2 C	472 g	Warm Water (120°~130°F)
5⅔ C	680 g	Bread Flour (approx)
3 TBS	38 g	Sugar or Malt (syrup or powder)
1 TBS	10 g	Instant Yeast
1 TBS	10 g	Salt (DC kosher)
1 large	19 g	Egg Yolk
1 large	30 g	Egg White for egg wash
1 TBS	15 g	Water for egg wash
1 TBS	9 g	Poppy or Sesame Seeds (optional)
2 oz	57 g	Asiago Cheese, grated (optional)

- Measure warm water into a large mixing bowl.
- Mix in 1 TBS of sugar and 3 C of flour; stir briskly until smooth.
- With batter temperature under 110°F, mix in yeast.
- Optionally, let batter rest 15~30 minutes (autolyse) while sponge develops.
- Mix in salt and egg yolk; mix in 2 C of flour, one at a time.
- Mix in additional flour, ¼ C at a time, until dough starts to release from bowl.
- Dust dough and counter lightly with flour and turn dough out.
- Knead until dough is smooth and elastic, adding flour only as necessary.
- Rise, covered, in a lightly oiled bowl until doubled in bulk.
- Fold dough on itself a few times; knead briefly; divide in half.
- Divide each half of dough into 6 pieces (or 5 for larger bagels).
- Form each piece into a ball; poke hole in center.
- Gradually enlarge hole to shape like a donut.
- Let rings rise 15~20 minutes, covered, on floured board.
- While rings rise, boil 2 inches of water in wide pot & preheat oven to 400°F.
- Lightly oil two sheet pans.
- Add 2 TBS of sugar to boiling water and mix in.
- Boil up to 3 rings at a time for 1~2 minutes per side.
- Drain in slotted spoon; put drained rings on prepared pans.
- Brush with egg white beaten with 1 TBS of water.
- Sprinkle with seeds, cheese, or other toppings if desired.
- Bake 25~30 minutes until golden brown and done.
- Transfer to a wire rack to cool before storing.

> **Recipe Tip**
> Try these toasted with smoked salmon and cream cheese.

LIGHT RYE BAGELS

1 C	236 g	Water, boiling
1 tsp	3 g	Caraway Seeds
1 tsp	3 g	Fennel Seeds, crushed
¼ C	55 g	Oil (or melted butter)
¼ C	59 g	Cider Vinegar
1 C	236 g	Cool Water (or OJ)
4 tsp	12 g	Instant Yeast
½ tsp	1 g	Cardamom, ground
4 tsp	12 g	Salt (DC kosher)
2 C	240 g	Rye Flour
4 C	480 g	Bread Flour (approx)

- Boil seeds for 5 minutes.
- Pour hot liquid with seeds into a large mixing bowl.
- Mix in oil, vinegar and cold water (in order!)
- Mix in 3 C of bread flour; beat well.
- With batter temperature under 110°F, mix in yeast and stir well.
- Optionally, let batter rest 15~30 minutes (autolyse) while sponge develops.
- Mix in cardamom and salt.
- Mix in rye flour, one cup at a time.
- Mix in additional bread flour, ¼ C at a time, until dough releases from bowl.
- Dust dough and counter lightly with bread flour and turn dough out.
- Knead until dough is smooth and elastic, adding flour only as necessary.
- Rise, covered, in a lightly oiled bowl until doubled in bulk.
- Fold dough on itself a few times; knead briefly; divide in half.
- Lightly oil two sheet pans.
- Form each piece into a ball; poke hole in center.
- Gradually enlarge hole to shape like a donut.
- Let rings rise 15~20 minutes, covered, on floured board.
- While rings rise, boil 2 inches of water in wide pot & preheat oven to 400°F.
- Boil up to 3 rings at a time for 1~2 minutes per side.
- Drain in slotted spoon; put drained rings on prepared pans.
- Bake 25~30 minutes until done.
- Transfer to a wire rack to cool before storing.

> **Recipe Tip**
> Try adding 1 TBS orange peel or fresh-grated zest for even more depth of flavor.

PUMPED-UP BAGELS

1 C	236 g	Boiling Hot Water
1 TBS	5 g	Instant Coffee or Instant Espresso Powder
1 TBS	9 g	Caraway Seeds (optional)
¼ C	60 g	Brown Sugar
¼ C	55 g	Oil (or melted butter)
¼ C	80 g	Molasses
¼ C	59 g	Cider Vinegar
¾ C	177 g	Cool Water
4 tsp	12 g	Instant Yeast
4 tsp	12 g	Salt (DC kosher)
3 TBS	16 g	Cocoa, unsweetened
½ C	60 g	Whole Wheat Flour
2 C	240 g	Rye Flour
3¾ C	450 g	Bread Flour (approx)
1 tsp	3 g	Cornstarch dissolved in ¼ C cold water

- Dissolve instant coffee in hot water in a large mixing bowl.
- Stir in seeds (if desired), sugar, oil, molasses, vinegar and cool water.
- Mix in 3 C of bread flour; beat well.
- With batter temperature under 110°F, mix in yeast.
- Optionally, let batter rest 15~30 minutes (autolyse) while sponge develops.
- Mix in salt and cocoa.
- Mix in whole wheat flour and then rye, one cup at a time.
- Mix in additional bread flour, ¼ C at a time, until dough releases from bowl.
- Dust dough and counter lightly with bread flour and turn dough out.
- Knead until dough is smooth and elastic, adding flour only as necessary.
- Rise, covered, in a lightly oiled bowl until doubled in bulk.
- Fold dough on itself a few times; knead briefly; divide in half.
- Divide each half of dough into 6 pieces (or 5 for larger bagels).
- Form each piece into a ball; poke hole in center.
- Gradually enlarge hole to shape like a donut.
- Let rings rise 15~20 minutes, covered, on floured board.
- While rings rise, boil 2 inches of water in wide pot & preheat oven to 400°F.
- Lightly oil two sheet pans.
- Boil up to 3 rings at a time for 1~2 minutes per side.
- Drain in slotted spoon; put drained rings on prepared pans.
- Bake 25~30 minutes until done.
- Bring cornstarch/water mix to a boil; brush bagels 10 minutes before done.
- Transfer to a wire rack to cool before storing.

CRANBERRY ORANGE SCONES

2 C	240 g	All-Purpose Flour
3 TBS	38 g	Sugar
½ tsp	2 g	Salt (DC kosher)
2½ tsp	12 g	Baking Powder
5 TBS	75 g	Butter, frozen (⅓ C)
½–¾ C	80~120 g	Sweetened Dried Cranberries
2 TBS	12 g	Zest of 1 Orange (or 1~2 tsp extract)
1 large	50 g	Egg, beaten
½ C	116 g	Cream or Half & Half

- Preheat oven to 400°F while you proceed with the recipe.
- Prepare sheet pan with parchment.

Make Dough
- Combine flour, sugar, salt, and baking powder in a mixing bowl.
- Grate butter into flour mixture.
- Mix in cranberries and orange.
- In a small bowl, beat egg; whisk in cream to mix.
- Stir cream and egg mixture (as required) into flour mixture to moisten.
- Be careful to not add more liquid than necessary!
- Knead gently on floured surface 5~10 times (less than 1 minute).

Shape & Bake
- Pat or roll to a form a ½-inch thick round disk.
- Cut disk into 8 pie shaped wedges.
- Place wedges on prepared pan.
- Optionally, brush tops with cream (or melted butter) and sprinkle with sugar.
- Bake 18~20 minutes until golden and just done (test with toothpick).
- Enjoy warm or cool on a wire rack before storing.

LEMON CREAM BLUEBERRY SCONES

2 C	240 g	All-Purpose Flour
¼ C	50 g	Sugar
1 tsp	3 g	Salt (DC kosher)
1 TBS	14 g	Baking Powder
½–¾ C	80~120 g	Sweetened Dried Blueberries
1 TBS	6 g	Zest of 1 Lemon (or 1~2 tsp extract)
1¼ C	290 g	Heavy Cream

- Preheat oven to 400°F while you proceed with the recipe.
- Prepare sheet pan with parchment.
- Combine flour, sugar, salt, and baking powder in a mixing bowl.
- Mix in blueberries and lemon.
- Stir cream (as required) into flour mixture to moisten.
- Be careful to not add more cream than necessary!
- Knead gently on floured surface 5~10 times (less than 1 minute).
- Shape same as Cranberry-Orange scones.
- Optionally, brush tops with cream (or melted butter) and sprinkle with sugar.
- Bake 18~20 minutes until golden and just done (test with toothpick).

CHOCOLATE CHIP SCONES

2 large	100 g	Eggs
¾ C	174 g	Heavy Cream
1 tsp	4 g	Vanilla
2½ C	300 g	All-Purpose Flour
5 TBS	75 g	Butter, frozen (⅓ C)
2 TBS	25 g	Sugar
½ tsp	2 g	Salt (DC kosher)
4 tsp	18 g	Baking Powder
1 C	180 g	Chocolate Chips

> **Recipe Tip**
> Substitute cinnamon baking chips in this recipe for great flavor.

- Preheat oven to 400°F while you proceed with the recipe.
- Prepare sheet pan with parchment.
- In a medium bowl, beat eggs; whisk in cream and vanilla.
- In a larger bowl, mix sugar, salt, baking powder, and chips into flour.
- Grate butter into flour mixture.
- Add cream and egg mixture (as required) to flour mixture and stir to combine.
- Be careful to not add more liquid than necessary!
- Knead gently on floured surface 5~10 times (less than 1 minute).
- Shape same as Cranberry-Orange scones.
- Optionally, brush tops with cream (or melted butter) and sprinkle with sugar.
- Bake 18~20 minutes until golden and just done (test with toothpick).

CRANBERRY ORANGE MUFFINS

2 C	240 g	All-Purpose Flour
¾ C	150 g	Sugar
1 tsp	3 g	Salt (DC kosher)
½ tsp	3 g	Baking Soda
2 tsp	9 g	Baking Powder
¾ C	120 g	Sweetened Dried Cranberries
2 TBS	12 g	Zest of 1 Orange (or 1~2 tsp extract)
1 large	50 g	Egg, beaten
¾ C	177 g	Orange Juice
¼ C	56 g	Vegetable Oil

- Preheat oven to 400°F while you proceed with the recipe.
- Combine flour, sugar, salt, baking soda and powder in a large bowl.
- Mix cranberries and zest into dry ingredients.
- In a small bowl, beat egg; mix in juice, and oil.
- Mix wet ingredients into dry ingredients.
- Spoon batter into greased or paper-lined muffin cups.
- Bake ~20 minutes until done (test with toothpick).
- Cool briefly on a wire rack before enjoying.

APPLE CINNAMON CHIP MUFFINS

2 C	240 g	All-Purpose Flour
¾ C	150 g	Sugar
2 tsp	9 g	Baking Powder
1 tsp	3 g	Salt (DC kosher)
1 tsp	5 g	Cinnamon
2 large	100 g	Eggs, beaten
½ C	122 g	Milk
¼ C	113 g	Applesauce
¼ C	56 g	Vegetable Oil
1 tsp	4 g	Vanilla Extract
1 C	170 g	Cinnamon Chips

- Preheat oven to 400°F while you proceed with the recipe.
- Combine flour, sugar, baking powder, salt, and cinnamon in a large bowl.
- In a small bowl, beat eggs; mix in milk, applesauce, oil, and vanilla.
- Mix wet ingredients into dry ingredients.
- Lastly, stir in chips.
- Spoon batter into greased or paper-lined muffin cups.
- Bake ~20 minutes until done (test with toothpick).
- Cool briefly on a wire rack before enjoying.

BAKING POWDER BISCUITS

2 C	240 g	All-Purpose Flour
1 TBS	14 g	Baking Powder
1 tsp	3 g	Salt (DC kosher)
2 tsp	8 g	Sugar (optional)
4 TBS	48 g	Cold Butter or Shortening
¾ C	183 g	Milk (approx)

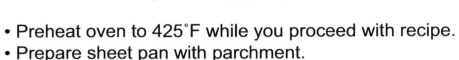

- Preheat oven to 425°F while you proceed with recipe.
- Prepare sheet pan with parchment.
- In a large bowl, mix flour, baking powder, salt, and sugar.
- Cut in butter with a pastry blender; add milk, stir only enough to mix well.
- Turn out onto a floured counter and knead very briefly.
- Roll out to ½ ~ ¾ inch thick (thick for fluffy, thin for crispy).
- Cut into 2½-inch disks with a biscuit cutter, inverted glass or clean tin can.
- Place on a prepared sheet pan, close for fluffy or spaced for crispy.
- Bake 12~14 minutes until biscuits are golden brown and done.
- Transfer to a cooling rack for a few minutes before enjoying warm.

SIMPLE DROP BISCUITS
so easy a cave man could make them

2 C	240 g	Self-Rising Flour
1⅓ C	309 g	Heavy Cream (approx)

- Preheat oven to 425°F & prepare sheet pan with parchment.
- In a large bowl, fold cream into flour and stir briefly to form a dough.
- Drop by ¼ C scoops onto prepared pan and bake 12~14 minutes until golden.

SWEET DESSERT BISCUITS
ideal for strawberry shortcake

basic recipe		Baking Powder Biscuits OR Cream Biscuits above
3 TBS	38 g	Sugar, mixed with dry ingredients
1 tsp	4 g	Vanilla Extract, mixed with wet ingredients

- Preheat oven to 425°F & prepare sheet pan with parchment.
- In a large bowl, mix dry ingredients well; mix wet ingredients separately.
- Fold wet ingredients into dry; adjust amount to make a soft dough.
- Knead briefly, roll out, cut into 3-inch disks, and bake to barely golden.
- Transfer to a cooling rack ~ 15 minutes before cutting in half for shortcakes.

SIMPLE SODA BREAD
Quick Skillet Bread

3 C	360 g	All-Purpose Flour
2 TBS	25 g	Sugar (optional)
1 TBS	14 g	Baking Powder
2 tsp	7 g	DC Kosher Salt
2 TBS	28 g	Butter
1½ C	366 g	Milk

> **Recipe Tip**
> To simplify, use self-rising flour & eliminate baking powder and salt.

- Preheat oven to 425°F while you proceed with the recipe.
- Combine dry ingredients in a large mixing bowl.
- Measure butter into an 8-inch non-stick skillet.
- Warm skillet on stove to melt butter; brush pan; pour off excess into milk.
- Gently mix milk and butter into dry ingredients until a stiff batter forms.
- Transfer batter to prepared pan.
- Dust top lightly with flour.
- Cut a 1-inch deep cross in the top with a serrated knife.
- Bake 35~40 minutes until done (test with toothpick).
- Remove from pan; cool on a wire rack before cutting or storing.

BEER BREAD
Quick Loaf Bread

3 C	360 g	All-Purpose Flour
3 TBS	38 g	Sugar
1 TBS	14 g	Baking Powder
2 tsp	7 g	DC Kosher Salt
¾ C	85 g	Cheddar Cheese, grated (optional)
1½ C	355 ml	Beer (12-ounce can/bottle)
4 TBS	57 g	Butter, melted

> **Recipe Tip**
> Experiment with different styles of beer and types of cheese.

- Preheat oven to 375°F while you proceed with the recipe.
- Butter a non-stick 8½ x 4½-inch loaf pan.
- Combine dry ingredients in a large mixing bowl.
- Gently mix beer and 2 TBS butter into dry ingredients; do not over-mix!
- Transfer batter to prepared pan.
- Bake 30 minutes.
- Brush top with remaining 2 TBS butter.
- Bake an additional 20~25 minutes until done (test with toothpick).
- Remove from pan; cool on a wire rack before cutting or storing.

CORN BREAD

1 C	120 g	Yellow Corn Meal
1 C	120 g	All-Purpose Flour
¼ C	50 g	Sugar
1 TBS	14 g	Baking Powder
2 tsp	6 g	DC Kosher Salt
1 large	50 g	Egg, beaten
1 C	244 g	Milk
¼ C	55 g	Oil (or melted butter/margarine)

- Preheat oven to 425°F while you proceed with the recipe.
- Grease a 9-inch skillet (or 8 x 8-inch pan).
- Combine dry ingredients in a large mixing bowl.
- Combine wet ingredients separately.
- Quickly mix wet ingredients into dry ingredients; do not over-mix!
- Bake 20~25 minutes until done (test with toothpick).
- Remove from pan; cool on a wire rack before cutting or storing.

> **Recipe Tip**
> This is a great bread to serve with chili.

BANANA BREAD

2 C	240 g	All-Purpose Flour
1 tsp	3 g	Salt (DC kosher)
2 tsp	9 g	Baking Powder
½ tsp	3 g	Baking Soda
½ C	113 g	Butter, softened
1 C	200 g	Sugar
2 large	100 g	Eggs, beaten
1 tsp	4 g	Vanilla Extract
⅓ C	81 g	Milk
1 tsp	5 g	Lemon Juice
2 large	300 g	Very Ripe Bananas
½ C	58 g	Walnuts, chopped (optional) OR
½ C	90 g	Chocolate Chips (optional)

> **Recipe Tip**
> You can freeze overripe bananas until you need them for this recipe.

- Preheat oven to 350°F while you proceed with the recipe.
- Combine flour, salt, baking powder and soda in a small bowl.
- In a large bowl, cream butter with sugar until light and fluffy.
- Beat in egg and vanilla.
- Stir lemon juice into milk, mash in bananas, and mix with butter/eggs.
- Mix dry ingredients (from small bowl) into wet ingredients, blending well.
- Lastly, mix in nuts or chocolate chips, if desired.
- Pour batter into a well-greased loaf pan (non-stick preferred).
- Bake ~1 hour until done (test with toothpick).
- Tent with foil halfway through baking to prevent a dark crust.
- Cool briefly in the pan and then on a wire rack before cutting or storing.

DATE NUT BREAD

1½ C	180 g	All-Purpose Flour
1 C	175 g	Dates (about 24 whole, pitted)
½ C	60 g	Whole Wheat Flour
1 tsp	3 g	Salt (DC kosher)
1 tsp	5 g	Baking Powder
1 tsp	5 g	Baking Soda
1 C	116 g	Walnuts
2 large	100 g	Eggs, beaten
4 TBS	57 g	Butter (½ stick)
¾ C	177 g	Coffee (hot brewed)
1 tsp	4 g	Vanilla Extract
¾ C	164 g	Brown Sugar

> **Recipe Tip**
> Processing dates in flour prevents clumping. Otherwise chop by hand.

- Preheat oven to 350°F while you proceed with the recipe.
- Grease a 8½ x 4½-inch loaf pan (non-stick preferred).
- Measure A-P flour into the workbowl of a food processor; add dates.
- Pulse motor to chop dates into raisin-size pieces; transfer to a large bowl.
- Measure W-W flour, salt, baking powder, soda, and nuts into the workbowl.
- Pulse motor to chop nuts coarsely; transfer to large bowl with dates.
- Break eggs into the workbowl; pulse motor to beat eggs briefly.
- Melt butter in hot coffee; add with vanilla and brown sugar to eggs.
- Pulse motor to dissolve the brown sugar in the warm liquid.
- Fold wet ingredients into dry ingredients, blending completely.
- Transfer the batter into the prepared loaf pan.
- Bake ~ 50 minutes until done (test with a toothpick); do not overbake.
- Tent pan with foil halfway through baking to prevent a dark crust.
- Cool briefly in the pan and then on a wire rack before cutting or storing.

BOSTON BROWN BREAD

1 TBS	14 g	Butter or Shortening for greasing can
½ C	65 g	Yellow Corn Meal
½ C	60 g	Whole Wheat Flour
½ C	60 g	Rye Flour
½ tsp	2 g	Baking Powder
½ tsp	2 g	Baking Soda
1 tsp	3 g	DC Kosher Salt
½ C	80 g	Raisins (optional)
1 C	244 g	Milk
⅓ C	107 g	Molasses

> **Recipe Tips**
> Bake the beans while the bread steams. Add some good hot dogs and dinner is all done!

- Preheat oven to 325°F while you proceed with the recipe.
- Fill a deep stock pot half full with water and heat to boiling.
- Grease an empty and clean 28-ounce baked bean can.
- Combine all dry ingredients in a large bowl and mix well.
- Mix in milk; then mix in molasses.
- Transfer batter into prepared can which should be ~ ⅔ full.
- Seal the can with a double-layer of heavy aluminum foil.
- Secure the foil on the can with several wraps of string and a good knot.
- Lower the can into the stock pot; the can should be half submerged.
- Put the lid on the pot and place it on a rack in the middle of the oven.
- Steam the bread for 1½ ~ 2 hours.
- Lift the can from the water bath and remove the foil.
- Let it cool for 45-60 minutes before removing the loaf from the can.

WHOLE WHEAT BATTER BREAD

1 TBS	12 g	Shortening to grease pan
2 C	240 g	Whole Wheat Flour
¼ C	17 g	Instant Dry Milk
1 TBS	10 g	Salt (DC kosher)
1½ C	354 g	Very Warm Water (140°F)
¼ C	80 g	Honey or Molasses (or 2 TBS ea)
2 TBS	28 g	Softened Butter
2 TBS	27 g	Vegetable Oil
1 TBS	10 g	Instant Yeast
1½ C	180 g	All-Purpose Flour

- Preheat oven to 375°F while you proceed with the recipe.
- Grease a large loaf pan OR muffin tin for rolls.
- Put W/W flour, milk, and salt into mixer work bowl.
- Separately, combine water, honey/molasses, butter, and oil.
- Heat liquids to 120°F.
- With mixer running, pour in liquids.
- With mixer running, add yeast.
- Optionally, let batter rest 15~30 minutes (autolyse) while sponge develops.
- With mixer running, add A-P flour to create a stiff batter.
- Beat 2 minutes at medium-high speed.
- For bread, transfer batter to loaf pan.
- For rolls, transfer an overflowing tablespoon of batter to a floured surface.
- Then roll to form a ball, and place ball in muffin tin well; repeat.
- Spray tops lightly with release (PAM) and cover.
- Rise approximately 45~55 minutes until almost but not quite double in bulk.
- Bake loaf ~45 minutes OR bake rolls ~20 minutes until done.
- Remove from pan; cool on a wire rack before cutting or storing.

Recipe Tip

- King Arthur whole wheat flour is "traditionally milled" with a finer texture than stone-ground wheat. This may help prevent the bran from cutting gluten strands as they form and result in bread that's not so dense.

WHITE WHOLE WHEAT SANDWICH BREAD

2 C	472 g	Warm Water (120°~130°F)
⅓ C	23 g	Instant Dry Milk
¼ C	50 g	Sugar (or Honey)
2 C	240 g	White Whole Wheat Flour
1 TBS	10 g	Instant Yeast
¼ C	55 g	Oil (or melted butter/margarine)
1 TBS	10 g	Salt (DC kosher)
2 C	240 g	Bread Flour
1¾ C	210 g	All-Purpose Flour (approx)
1 TBS	11 g	Semolina for dusting pans

- Measure warm water into a large mixing bowl.
- Mix in milk, sugar, and whole wheat flour; stir briskly until smooth.
- With batter temperature under 110°F, mix in yeast.
- Optionally, let batter rest 15~30 minutes (autolyse) while sponge develops.
- Mix in oil and salt.
- Mix in bread flour, one cup at a time.
- Mix in A-P flour, ¼ C at a time, until dough starts to release from bowl.
- Dust dough and counter lightly with flour and turn dough out.
- Knead until dough is smooth and elastic, adding flour only as necessary.
- Rise, covered, in a lightly oiled bowl until doubled in bulk.
- Lightly spray two loaf pans with release (PAM) and sprinkle with semolina.
- Fold dough on itself a few times; knead briefly; divide in half.
- Shape into loaves and place in prepared baking pans.
- Rise, covered, until almost doubled.
- Preheat oven to 375°F while dough rises.
- Lightly dust tops of loaves with flour; slash tops with one long stroke.
- Bake 30~35 minutes until done.
- Remove from pans; cool on a wire rack before cutting or storing.

WHOLE GRAIN

Recipe Tip

White whole wheat flour is a great way to get more healthy fiber into your family's diet without them even knowing! You can bump the percentage of whole wheat up as you learn how to work with whole grains.

WHOLE WHEAT CINNAMON SWIRL BREAD

1½	366 g	Milk, scalded
1 C	160 g	Dark Raisins (optional)
⅓ C	73 g	Oil (or melted butter/margarine)
⅓ C	107 g	Molasses
2 TBS	30 g	Brown Sugar
1 large	19 g	Egg yolk (reserve white)
1 large	50 g	Egg (whole), beaten
3 C	360 g	Whole Wheat Flour
4 tsp	13 g	Instant Yeast
4 tsp	13 g	Salt (DC kosher)
2½ C	300 g	Bread Flour (approx)
1 large	30 g	Egg white (reserved)
2 TBS	42 g	Honey (as required)
2 TBS	10 g	Cinnamon (as required)

Recipe Tip
Go light on the honey and heavy on the cinnamon.

- Scald milk in saucepan or microwave to 180°F.
- Plump raisins, if desired, in hot milk ~ 3 minutes.
- Add oil, molasses and sugar to the milk; stir to mix.
- In a large bowl, beat egg yolk and whole egg together.
- Stir milk/oil/molasses/sugar mixture into beaten eggs (temper).
- Beat in whole wheat flour, one cup at a time.
- With batter temperature under 110°F, mix in yeast.
- Optionally, let batter rest 15~30 minutes (autolyse) while sponge develops.
- Mix in salt and 2 C of bread flour, one at a time.
- Mix in additional bread flour, ¼ C at a time, until dough just releases from bowl.
- Dust dough and counter lightly with flour and turn dough out.
- Knead until dough is smooth and elastic, adding flour only as necessary.
- Rise, covered, in a lightly oiled bowl until doubled in bulk.
- Fold dough on itself a few times; knead briefly; divide in half.
- Cover and rest 10~15 minutes.
- While dough rests, mix 2 TBS honey into reserved egg white.
- Line bottoms of two loaf pans with parchment; butter sides.
- Roll out each half to a rectangle 7 inches wide x 16 inches deep.
- Spread with thin layer of honey mix, leaving a half-inch border around outside.
- Sprinkle heavily with cinnamon.
- Roll up from far short edge towards you; pinch seams and ends to seal.
- Place loaves in prepared pans with seam side down.
- Rise, covered, until almost but not quite doubled.
- Preheat oven to 375°F while dough rises.
- Bake 35~40 minutes until done.
- Remove from pans; cool on a wire rack before cutting or storing.

GOLDEN FLAX BREAD

1¾ C	413 g	Warm Water (130°F)
¼ C	17 g	Instant Dry Milk
⅓ C	107 g	Molasses
4 tsp	11 g	Instant Yeast
⅓ C	73 g	Oil (or melted butter/margarine)
4 TBS	26 g	Milled Flax Seed
4 tsp	11 g	Salt (DC kosher)
6 C	720 g	All-Purpose Flour (approx)
1 TBS	11 g	Cornmeal or Semolina for pans

- Measure warm water into a large mixing bowl.
- Mix in milk, molasses and 3 C of flour; beat well.
- With batter temperature under 110°F, mix in yeast.
- Optionally, let batter rest 15~30 minutes (autolyse) while sponge develops.
- Mix in oil, flax, and salt.
- Beat in 2 C of flour, one at a time.
- Mix in additional flour, ¼ C at a time, until dough starts to release from bowl.
- Dust dough and counter lightly with flour and turn dough out.
- Knead until dough is smooth and elastic, adding flour only as necessary.
- Rise, covered, in a lightly oiled bowl until doubled in bulk.
- Fold dough on itself a few times; knead briefly; divide in half.
- Shape dough into loaves.
- Lightly grease two loaf pans and sprinkle with cornmeal or semolina.
- Place dough in prepared pans and rise, covered, until almost doubled.
- Preheat oven to 375°F while dough rises.
- Bake ~ 35 minutes until done.
- Remove from pans; cool on a wire rack before cutting or storing.

Recipe Tip

Flax gives bread a healthy nutritional boost with omega-3 essential fatty acids, lignans, and fiber.

TRADITIONAL OATMEAL BREAD

2 C	472 g	Boiling Water (or scalded milk)
1½ C	120 g	Rolled Oats (old fashioned or quick)
⅓ C	107 g	Molasses (or dark corn syrup or honey)
4 tsp	13 g	Instant Yeast
⅓ C	73 g	Oil (or melted butter)
4 tsp	13 g	Salt (DC kosher)
2 TBS	15 g	Vital Wheat Gluten (optional)
5¼ C	630 g	Bread Flour (approx)
½ C	39 g	Rolled Oats for outside

> **Recipe Tip**
> Allow sufficient time for the oatmeal to cool. This can take up to an hour.

- Pour hot liquid over oatmeal in large mixing bowl, stir, allow to cool.
- With batter temperature under 110°F, mix in molasses and yeast.
- Optionally, let batter rest 15~30 minutes (autolyse) while sponge develops.
- Mix in oil, salt, and gluten.
- Beat in 4 C of flour, one at a time.
- Mix in additional flour, ¼ C at a time, until dough starts to release from bowl.
- Dust dough and counter lightly with flour and turn dough out.
- Knead until dough is smooth and elastic, adding flour only as necessary.
- Rise, covered, in a lightly oiled bowl until doubled in bulk.
- Fold dough on itself a few times; knead briefly; divide in half.
- Shape dough into loaves; rolled and sealed logs work well.
- Roll each loaf in oats to coat evenly.
- Place loaves in non-stick or lightly oiled loaf pans.
- Rise, covered, until almost but not quite doubled.
- Preheat oven to 375°F while dough rises.
- Bake 35~40 minutes until done.
- Remove from pans; cool on a wire rack before cutting or storing.

QUICK & EASY OATMEAL BREAD

1½ C	120 g	Rolled Oats (or 1 C + 1 TBS Oat Flour)
1¾ C	413 g	Warm Water (130°F)
⅓ C	23 g	Instant Dry Milk (optional)
⅓ C	107 g	Molasses (or honey)
4 TBS	26 g	Milled Flax Seed (optional)
4 tsp	13 g	Instant Yeast
⅓ C	75 g	Oil (or melted butter)
4 tsp	13 g	Salt (DC kosher)
5 C	600 g	Bread Flour (approx)
½ C	39 g	Rolled Oats for outside

- Use food processor to mill oats into flour.
- Combine water, milk, and molasses in a large mixing bowl.
- Mix in oat flour, flax seed, and 1½ C of bread flour; beat well.
- With batter temperature under 110°F, mix in yeast.
- Optionally, let batter rest 15~30 minutes (autolyse) while sponge develops.
- Mix in oil, salt, and 3 C of bread flour, one at a time.
- Mix in additional flour, ¼ C at a time, until dough starts to release from bowl.
- Dust dough and counter lightly with flour and turn dough out.
- Knead until dough is smooth and elastic, adding flour only as necessary.
- Rise, covered, in a lightly oiled bowl until doubled in bulk.
- Fold dough on itself a few times; knead briefly; divide in half.
- Shape into loaves; tightly rolled and sealed logs work well.
- Roll each loaf in oats to coat evenly.
- Place loaves in non-stick or lightly oiled loaf pans.
- Rise, covered, until almost but not quite doubled.
- Preheat oven to 375°F while dough rises.
- Bake 35~40 minutes until done.
- Remove from pans; cool on a wire rack before cutting or storing.

Recipe Tip

- Since oats do not contain the proteins that produce gluten, this recipe contains bread flour to help with gluten development.

CANADIAN STYLE BROWN BREAD

1¾ C	413 g	Warm Water (130°F)
½ C	35 g	Instant Dry Milk
¼ C	60 g	Brown Sugar
¼ C	80 g	Molasses
1 TBS	10 g	Instant Yeast
¼ C	55 g	Oil (or melted butter/margarine)
1 TBS	10 g	Salt (DC kosher)
1 C	104 g	Oat Flour
1 C	120 g	Whole Wheat Flour
3¼ C	390 g	Bread Flour (approx)
1 TBS	11 g	Cornmeal or Semolina for dusting pans

- Measure warm water into a large mixing bowl.
- Mix in milk, sugar, molasses and 3 C of bread flour; beat well.
- With batter temperature under 110°F, mix in yeast.
- Optionally, let batter rest 15~30 minutes (autolyse) while sponge develops.
- Mix in oil, salt and then the oat and whole wheat flours, one at a time.
- Mix in bread flour, ¼ C at a time, until dough starts to release from bowl.
- Dust dough and counter lightly with flour and turn dough out.
- Knead until dough is smooth and elastic, adding flour only as necessary.
- Rise, covered, in a lightly oiled bowl until doubled in bulk.
- Fold dough on itself a few times; knead briefly; divide in half.
- Spray loaf pans lightly with release (PAM); sprinkle with cornmeal or semolina.
- Shape dough into loaves and place in prepared pans.
- Rise, covered, until almost doubled.
- Preheat oven to 375°F while dough rises.
- Bake ~ 35 minutes until done.
- Remove from pans; cool on a wire rack before cutting or storing.

Recipe Tip
- Whole wheat is often called brown bread in Canada. This one is sweetened with oats, molasses, and brown sugar. It is nice and light and perfect for sandwiches.

LIGHT RYE BREAD

2¼ C	531 g	Warm Water (120°~130°F)
2 TBS	30 g	Brown Sugar
4 tsp	13 g	Instant Yeast
4 tsp	13 g	Salt (DC kosher)
1½ TBS	13 g	Caraway Seeds
2 TBS	12 g	Zest of 1 Orange
¼ C	55 g	Oil (or melted butter)
2 C	240 g	Rye Flour
4½ C	540 g	Bread Flour (approx)
1 TBS	11 g	Semolina for dusting pans

- Measure warm water and sugar into a large mixing bowl.
- Mix in 3 C of bread flour; stir briskly until smooth.
- With batter temperature under 110°F, mix in yeast.
- Optionally, let batter rest 15~30 minutes (autolyse) while sponge develops.
- Mix in salt, seeds (if desired), orange, and oil.
- Mix in rye flour, one cup at a time.
- Mix in bread flour, ¼ C at a time, until dough starts to release from bowl.
- Dust dough and counter lightly with bread flour and turn dough out.
- Knead until dough is smooth and elastic, adding flour only as necessary.
- Rise, covered, in a lightly oiled bowl until doubled in bulk.
- Fold dough on itself a few times; knead briefly; divide in half.
- Prepare sheet pan with parchment (optional).
- Sprinkle pan with semolina.
- Shape dough into loaves and place on prepared pan.
- Rise dough, covered, until almost but not quite doubled.
- Preheat oven to 400°F while dough rises.
- Dust loaves with rye and slash just before baking.
- Bake ~ 35 minutes until done.
- Remove from pan; cool on a wire rack before cutting or storing.

> **Recipe Tip**
> - Caraway seeds aren't for everyone!
> If you don't like them, leave them out.

PUMPERNICKEL

¼ C	59 g	Boiling Hot Water
1 TBS	5 g	Instant Coffee
1½ C	354 g	Warm Water (120°~130°F)
¼ C	55 g	Oil (or melted butter)
¼ C	80 g	Molasses
¼ C	59 g	Cider Vinegar
4 tsp	13 g	Instant Yeast
4 tsp	13 g	Salt (DC kosher)
3 TBS	16 g	Cocoa, unsweetened
1 TBS	9 g	Caraway Seeds (optional)
½ C	60 g	Whole Wheat Flour
2 C	240 g	Rye Flour
3¾ C	450 g	Bread Flour (approx)
1 TBS	11 g	Cornmeal or Semolina for dusting pans
1 tsp	3 g	Cornstarch dissolved in ¼ C cold water

- Pour hot water over instant coffee in a large mixing bowl; stir to dissolve.
- Stir in warm water.
- Mix in oil, molasses, vinegar, and 3 C of bread flour; beat well.
- With batter temperature under 110°F, mix in yeast.
- Optionally, let batter rest 15~30 minutes (autolyse) while sponge develops.
- Mix in salt, cocoa, and seeds (if desired).
- Beat in whole wheat flour and then rye flour, one cup at a time.
- Mix in bread flour, ¼ C at a time, until dough starts to release from bowl.
- Dust dough and counter lightly with bread flour and turn dough out.
- Knead until dough is smooth and elastic, adding flour only as necessary.
- Rise, covered, in a lightly oiled bowl until doubled in bulk.
- Fold dough on itself a few times; knead briefly; divide in half.
- Prepare pan with parchment (optional).
- Sprinkle pan with cornmeal or semolina.
- Shape dough into loaves and place on prepared pan.
- Rise dough, covered, until almost but not quite doubled.
- If desired, constrict the diameter while rising for a higher/lighter loaf.
- Preheat oven to 375°F while dough rises.
- Dust loaves with rye and slash just before baking.
- Bake ~ 35 minutes until done.
- Bring cornstarch/water mix to a boil; brush loaves 10 minutes before done.
- Remove from pan; cool on a wire rack before cutting or storing.

MULTIGRAIN BREAD

1 C	236 g	Boiling Hot Water
1 C	160 g	Multi-Grain Hot Cereal
¾ C	183 g	Milk
¼ C	85 g	Honey
¼ C	80 g	Molasses
1½ C	180 g	Whole Wheat Flour
4 tsp	13 g	Instant Yeast
⅓ C	73 g	Oil (or melted butter)
4 tsp	13 g	Salt (DC kosher)
3 C	360 g	Bread Flour (approx)
½ C	39 g	Rolled Oats for outside

- Pour hot water over cereal in a large mixing bowl.
- Mix in milk, honey, and molasses; then mix in whole wheat flour.
- With batter temperature under 110°F, mix in yeast.
- Optionally, let batter rest 15~30 minutes (autolyse) while sponge develops.
- Mix in oil and salt.
- Beat in 2½ C of bread flour, one cup at a time.
- Mix in more bread flour, ¼ C at a time, until dough starts to release from bowl.
- Dust dough and counter lightly with bread flour and turn dough out.
- Knead until dough is smooth and elastic, adding flour only as necessary.
- Rise, covered, in a lightly oiled bowl until doubled in bulk.
- Fold dough on itself a few times; knead briefly; divide in half.
- Press dough out and roll into logs, sealing edges, or shape into round balls.
- Roll each loaf in oats to coat evenly.
- Place loaves in non-stick or lightly oiled loaf pans.
- Rise, covered, until almost but not quite doubled.
- Preheat oven to 375°F while dough rises.
- Bake ~ 40 minutes until done.
- Remove from pans.
- Cool on a wire rack before cutting or storing.

> **Recipe Tips**
>
> Try Bob's Red Mill 8-Grain hot cereal mix for this recipe. This blend is wheat-free, so adding whole wheat and bread flour produces a nice 9-grain bread. You can also use this recipe with rolled oats to make traditional oatmeal bread.

SOURDOUGH CULTURE

1	large bunch of "dusty" grapes
1 C	Pineapple juice
4 C	Whole Wheat or Bread Flour or 50/50 mix
	Chlorine-free Water

Day 1:
Buy a bunch of grapes which are covered with what looks like white dust. Do not wash them! Also buy some pineapple juice. Put the grapes in a bowl and pour enough pineapple juice over them to cover. Toss several times to rinse the yeast off of the grape skins. Strain the juice off into a small bowl. Eat the grapes for a snack! Stir enough flour into the juice to make a batter. Almost any good unbleached flour should work. Cover the bowl loosely with plastic wrap and allow to ferment on the counter at room temperature. Stir it up every few hours if you remember when you walk by it. This adds oxygen which encourages yeast growth while discouraging bacteria growth.

Day 2:
Watch for activity in the form of bubbles rising to the surface. Stir up the batter 2 or 3 times during the day. Re-cover your bowl loosely with wrap and continue to ferment at room temperature.

Days 3:
Continue to watch for activity in the form of bubbles rising to the surface. Stir up the batter 2 or 3 times during the day. Re-cover your bowl loosely with wrap and continue to ferment at room temperature. When you see some obvious activity you can proceed to the next step.

Days 4:
At this point your culture should be showing signs of activity. If so, proceed with the next step. If not, give it another day or two. Mix a quarter-cup of chlorine-free water into your culture. Then mix in a half-cup of flour. This will "feed" the culture. Re-cover your bowl loosely with plastic wrap and allow to ferment at room temperature.

Day 5:
Mix another quarter-cup of chlorine-free water into your culture. Then mix in a half-cup of flour. Re-cover your bowl loosely with wrap and continue to ferment at room temperature. The starter should be quite active at this point. If not, discard and start over with a fresh bunch of grapes.

Week 2:
This step will convert your culture into a mother starter that you will store in the fridge and use to make bread. The mother starter will be like a slightly sticky dough less salt. Transfer the culture to your mixer. Mix in 1 cup of chlorine-free water. This will turn it from dough to a batter. Mix in 2½ cups of flour. This will turn it back into a dough. Turn out onto a floured board and knead to bring it together and form a smooth dough. Transfer it to a container at least twice as large as the dough. Cover loosely with plastic wrap and allow to ferment on the counter at room temperature until double in bulk. Punch the dough down and transfer it the fridge. Punch it down each time it doubles. Growth should slow down after 8 hours in the fridge. You should warm and feed your starter several days before you plan to bake with it. To feed the starter simply repeat the steps in this paragraph again. It may take more than one feeding to re-activate a sleepy starter.

based on techniques by Peter Reinhardt

PAIN AU LEVAIN – AUTHENTIC SOURDOUGH
slow – leavened with starter only

1 C	275 g	Mother Starter (50% whole wheat)
1 C	236 g	Warm Chlorine-free Water (110°F)
3 C	360 g	All-Purpose Flour
2 tsp	6 g	Salt (DC kosher)
1 TBS	11 g	Semolina for dusting pans

> **Recipe Tip**
> This is not a fast-rise recipe. Allow time for wild yeast to leaven this bread.

- Bring starter to room temperature in a large mixing bowl.
- Mix warm chlorine-free water slowly into starter (temper).
- Mix in 1 C of flour to make a batter.
- Let batter rest for 30~60 minutes (autolyse) while sponge develops.
- Mix in salt.
- Beat in 1½ C of additional flour, ½ C at a time.
- Dust dough and counter with ¼ C of flour (reserve ¼ C).
- Turn dough out onto counter.
- Stretch and fold to knead; dough should be sticky inside; do not over flour.
- Rise, covered, in a warm place until doubled in bulk.
- Divide dough in half (for two 1# batches). Do not punch down; be gentle!
- Prepare sheet pan with parchment (optional); sprinkle pan with semolina.
- Shape by stretching and folding into loaves.
- Transfer shaped dough to prepared pan.
- Allow dough to rise until almost but not quite doubled in bulk.
- Preheat oven (and baking stone if available) to 475°F while dough rises.
- Just before baking, slash loaves quickly & diagonally with a serrated knife.
- Mist loaves with water before baking and twice more at 3-minute intervals.
- Bake to golden brown and a tap on the bottom sounds hollow, 20~25 minutes.
- Cool on a wire rack before cutting or storing.

SOURDOUGH FLAVORED BREAD
fast - leavened with commercial yeast

1 C	275 g	Mother Starter
1 C	236 g	Hot Water (180°F)
3 C	360 g	All-Purpose Flour
2 tsp	6 g	Instant Yeast
2 tsp	6 g	Salt (DC kosher)
1 TBS	11 g	Semolina for pan

- Bring starter to room temperature in a large mixing bowl.
- Mix hot water into starter.
- Mix in 1 C of flour to make a batter.
- With batter temperature under 110°F, mix in yeast.
- Let batter rest for 15~30 minutes (autolyse) while sponge develops.
- Mix in salt.
- Beat in 1½ C of additional flour, ½ C at a time.
- Dust dough and counter with ¼ C of flour (reserve ¼ C).
- Turn dough out onto counter.
- Stretch and fold to knead; dough should be sticky inside; do not over flour.
- Rise, covered, in a warm place until doubled in bulk, 30~40 minutes.
- Preheat oven (and baking stone if available) to 475°F while dough rises.
- Divide dough in half (for two 1# batches). Do not punch down; be gentle!
- Prepare sheet pan with parchment (optional); sprinkle pan with semolina.
- Shape by stretching and folding into loaves or rolls.
- Transfer shaped dough to prepared pan.
- Allow dough to rise until almost but not quite doubled, about 30 minutes.
- Just before baking, slash loaves quickly & diagonally with a serrated knife.
- Mist loaves with water before baking and twice more at 3-minute intervals.
- Bake until done ~30 minutes for bread or ~20 minutes for rolls.
- Cool on a wire rack before cutting or storing.

> **Recipe Tip**
> This is recipe uses starter for great sourdough flavor and instant yeast to speed up the rise.

JEWISH STYLE RYE
sourdough flavored - leavened with commercial yeast - pareve

1½ C	375 g	Mature Rye Starter
2 TBS	18 g	Caraway Seeds
1½ C	354 g	Boiling Hot Water
2 TBS	30 g	Brown Sugar
1 TBS	10 g	Instant Yeast
1 TBS	10 g	Salt (DC kosher)
4¾ C	570 g	Bread Flour (approx)
1 TBS	11 g	Semolina for pan
1 large	19 g	Egg Yolk for wash
1 TBS	15 g	Water for wash

- Bring starter to room temperature and feed the day before using.
- Transfer 1½ C of starter into a large mixing bowl; add caraway if desired.
- Measure hot water into bowl with starter and seeds; mix well.
- Mix in sugar and 1½ C bread flour to make a batter.
- With batter temperature under 110°F, mix in yeast.
- Let batter rest for 15~30 minutes (autolyse) while sponge develops.
- Mix in salt and then 3 C of bread flour, one at a time.
- Dust dough and counter with flour and turn out.
- Knead until dough forms a smooth ball, adding flour only as necessary.
- Rise, covered, in an oiled bowl until doubled in bulk.
- Prepare sheet pan with parchment (optional); sprinkle pan with semolina.
- Divide dough in half; do not punch down; be gentle!
- Shape each half of dough into a loaf or 10 equal size rolls.
- Transfer shaped dough to prepared pan; repeat with other half of dough.
- Allow dough to rise, covered, until almost but not quite doubled in bulk.
- Preheat oven (and baking stone if available) to 425°F while dough rises.
- Just before baking, slash loaves quickly & diagonally with a serrated knife.
- Beat egg with 1 TBS water and brush loaves/rolls just before baking.
- Bake until done ~35 minutes for loaves or ~20 minutes for rolls.
- Cool on a wire rack before cutting or storing.

> **Recipe Tips**
> This recipe uses boiling hot water to warm the starter and extract extra flavor from the caraway seeds.

PAPOSECOS
Portuguese Rolls

2 C	472 g	Warm Water (120°~130°F)
5½ C	660 g	All-Purpose Flour (approx)
1 TBS	13 g	Sugar
1 TBS	10 g	Instant Yeast
1 TBS	10 g	Salt (DC kosher)
1 TBS	13 g	Shortening or Lard
2 TBS	21 g	Semolina for dusting pans

- Measure warm water into a large mixing bowl.
- Mix in sugar and 3 C of flour; stir briskly until smooth.
- With batter temperature under 110°F, mix in yeast.
- Optionally, let batter rest 15~30 minutes (autolyse) while sponge develops.
- Mix in salt and shortening.
- Mix in 2 C of flour, one cup at a time.
- Mix in additional flour, ¼ C at a time, until dough starts to release from bowl.
- Dust dough and counter lightly with flour and turn dough out.
- Knead until dough is smooth and elastic, adding flour only as necessary.
- Rise, covered, in a lightly oiled bowl until doubled in bulk.
- Preheat oven to 450°F while dough rises.
- Prepare sheet pan with parchment (optional); sprinkle pan with semolina.
- Fold dough on itself a few times and knead briefly.
- Divide dough into 10~12 equal size pieces.
- Using palm of hand, roll pieces into balls and flatten into 4-inch rounds.
- Using edge of hand, make crease in middle of rounds.
- Fold sides in to middle and pinch ends to form slight points.
- Place rolls about 2-inches apart on prepared pan.
- Dust rolls lightly with flour.
- Rise, covered, until almost but not quite doubled, ~30 minutes.
- Bake 15~20 minutes until done.
- Rolls should sound hollow when tapped on bottom.
- Enjoy warm or cool on a wire rack before storing.

Recipe Tips

- This is a great simple recipe for beginners, and it makes authentic rolls. Make them any size you want; big ones are good for burger buns. Within a batch, however, shape them approximately the same size so they will all finish baking at the same time.

PORTUGUESE SWEET BREAD
Updated Authentic Recipe

1½ C	366 g	Milk, scalded
½ C	113 g	Butter/Margarine (1 stick)
1 C	200 g	Sugar
4 large	200 g	Eggs, beaten (reserve 1 white)
4 tsp	13 g	Instant Yeast (SAF Gold preferred)
1 TBS	10 g	Salt (DC kosher)
8 C	960 g	All-Purpose Flour (approx)

- Warm eggs in hot tap water while you continue.
- Scald milk in saucepan or microwave to 180°F.
- Add butter/margarine to hot milk to melt.
- Dissolve sugar in milk mixture.
- In a large bowl, beat eggs.
- Add milk mixture to beaten eggs.
- Mix in 3 C of flour; beat well by hand or with mixer.
- With batter temperature under 110°F, mix in yeast.
- Optionally, let batter rest 15~30 minutes (autolyse) while sponge develops.
- Mix in salt and then 4 additional C of flour, one cup at a time.
- Mix in more flour, ¼ C at a time, until dough starts to release from bowl.
- Dust dough and counter lightly with flour and turn dough out.
- Knead until dough is smooth and elastic, adding flour only as necessary.
- Rise, covered, in a lightly oiled bowl until doubled in bulk.
- Lightly grease the sides of 2 round casseroles or 9-inch cake pans.
- Line the bottom of the casseroles/pans with parchment cut to fit.
- Fold dough on itself a few times; knead briefly; divide in half.
- Shape dough into rounds; place into prepared casseroles/pans.
- Allow dough to rise, covered, until almost but not quite doubled.
- Preheat oven to 375°F while dough rises.
- Brush tops with egg white beaten with small amount of water.
- Bake 35~40 minutes until golden and done.
- Tent tops with foil if they appear to be browning too rapidly.
- Remove from casseroles; cool on a wire rack before cutting or storing.

INTERNATIONAL

SPANISH BREAD

Dough
2 large	100 g	Eggs, beaten
¾ C	183 g	Milk, scalded (180°F)
¼ C	57 g	Butter (half stick)
⅓ C	67 g	Sugar (plain)
2 tsp	7 g	Instant Yeast
2 tsp	7 g	Salt (DC kosher)
3⅔ C	440 g	All-Purpose Flour (approx)

Topping
¼ C	57 g	Butter, melted
½ C	56 g	Breadcrumbs
½ C	109 g	Brown Sugar

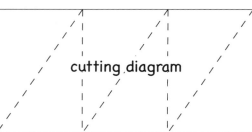

cutting diagram

- Beat eggs in a large mixing bowl.
- Scald milk in saucepan or microwave to 180°F.
- Add butter to hot milk; stir to melt.
- Mix plain sugar into hot milk.
- Stir milk mixture into beaten eggs (temper).
- Mix in 1½ C of flour; beat well by hand or with mixer.
- With batter temperature under 110°F, mix in yeast.
- Optionally, let batter rest 15~30 minutes (autolyse) while sponge develops.
- Mix in salt; then mix in 2 C of flour, 1 C at a time.
- Mix in additional flour, 2 TBS at a time, until dough releases from bowl.
- Dust dough and counter lightly with flour and turn dough out.
- Knead until dough is smooth and elastic, adding flour only as necessary.
- Rise, covered, in a lightly oiled bowl until doubled in bulk.
- Prepare two sheet pans with parchment.
- Mix breadcrumbs and brown sugar.
- Fold dough on itself a few times; knead briefly; divide in half.
- Roll dough out to a rectangle 12 inches wide x 6 inches tall.
- Brush with melted butter, sprinkle with breadcrumbs and brown sugar.
- Using a bench scraper, divide the rectangle in thirds about 4 inches wide.
- Divide each 4x6 rectangle in half along a diagonal forming triangles.
- Starting at the wide end, roll the triangles up ending with the point.
- Then coat the rolled dough with more breadcrumbs and sugar.
- Place formed buns with point down on the prepared pans.
- Allow buns to rise, covered, until puffy and almost doubled in size.
- Preheat oven to 350°F while dough rises.
- Bake ~18 minutes until golden and just done; do not over-bake.
- Remove from pans; cool briefly on a wire rack; enjoy warm.

ENSAÏMADAS
Mallorcan Sweet Rolls

2 large	100 g	Eggs, beaten
1¼ C	305 g	Milk, scalded (180°F)
½ C	100 g	Sugar
1 TBS	10 g	Instant Yeast
⅓ C	75 g	Vegetable Oil
2 tsp	7 g	Salt (DC kosher)
5 C	600 g	All-Purpose Flour (approx)
⅓ C	75 g	Butter or Lard for coating
¼ C	29 g	Confectioners' Sugar

- Beat eggs in a large mixing bowl.
- Scald milk in saucepan or microwave to 180°F.
- Mix sugar into hot milk.
- Stir milk mixture into beaten eggs (temper).
- Mix in 2 C of flour; beat well by hand or with mixer.
- With batter temperature under 110°F, mix in yeast.
- Optionally, let batter rest 15~30 minutes (autolyse) while sponge develops.
- Mix in oil and salt.
- Mix in 2 C of flour, one at a time.
- Mix in additional flour, ¼ C at a time, until dough releases from bowl.
- Dust dough and counter lightly with flour and turn dough out.
- Knead until dough is smooth and elastic, adding flour only as necessary.
- Rise, covered, in a lightly oiled bowl until doubled in bulk.
- Prepare two sheet pans with parchment.
- Fold dough on itself a few times; knead briefly; divide in half.
- Divide each half into 8 equal size pieces (about 70 g each).
- Roll pieces into 15-inch long ropes; surface should be smooth, not wrinkled.
- Coat each rope with melted butter/lard and create spiral snail-shaped buns.
- Take care to tuck the outer loose ends under the buns.
- Place formed buns on the prepared pans with plenty of space between.
- Allow buns to rise, covered, until doubled in size.
- Preheat oven to 350°F while dough rises.
- Bake 12~15 minutes until golden and just done; do not over-bake.
- Remove from pans; cool briefly on a wire rack.
- Dust with confectioners' sugar before serving warm.

> **Recipe Tip**
> Lard (saïm) is traditional, but butter can be used.

INTERNATIONAL

PROVENCAL FOUGASSE
French Flatbread

1¾ C	413 g	Warm Water (120°~130°F)
1 TBS	10 g	Instant Yeast
¼ C	55 g	Extra Virgin Olive Oil
3 cloves	3 g	Garlic, chopped
1 TBS	2 g	Fresh Rosemary, chopped
1 TBS	2 g	Fresh Oregano, chopped
1 TBS	2 g	Fresh Thyme, chopped
1 TBS	10 g	Salt (DC kosher)
5⅓ C	640 g	All-Purpose Flour (approx)
2 TBS	21 g	Semolina for dusting pans

- Measure warm water into a large mixing bowl.
- Mix in 2½ C of flour; stir briskly until smooth.
- With batter temperature under 110°F, mix in yeast.
- Let batter rest (autolyse) while you continue with the recipe.
- In small saucepan combine olive oil and herbs.
- Cook over medium heat until garlic is tender (about 1 minute).
- Allow oil / herbs to cool; add salt and mix into batter.
- Mix in 2 C of flour, one at a time.
- Mix in additional flour, ¼ C at a time, until dough starts to release from bowl.
- Dust dough and counter lightly with flour and turn dough out.
- Knead until dough is smooth and elastic, adding flour only as necessary.
- Rise, covered, in a lightly oiled bowl until doubled in bulk.
- Preheat oven to 425°F while dough rises.
- Prepare sheet pans with parchment (optional); sprinkle pans with semolina.
- Fold dough on itself a few times; knead briefly; divide in half.
- Allow dough to rest 5~10 minutes.
- Roll dough into rectangles (to just fit in sheet pans).
- Place dough on prepared pans.
- Cut 6 diagonal slits in dough (3 on each side); open slits to form ovals.
- Rise, covered, until almost but not quite doubled, about 20 minutes.
- Bake 15~20 minutes until golden and done.
- Enjoy warm or cool on a wire rack before storing.

Recipe Tip
In the day of community bakeries in rural France, each family had a unique pattern that distinguished their bread from others. Be creative!

PAIN DE CAMPAGNE
Traditional French Boule

Pâte Fermentée Preferment

¾ C	177 g	Lukewarm Water (85°F)
2 C	240 g	Bread Flour
1 tsp	3 g	Instant Yeast
1 tsp	3 g	Salt (DC kosher)

- Combine water and half of flour in mixer work bowl.
- Mix yeast thoroughly into batter; let batter rest 15 minutes.
- Mix in salt and remaining flour to create a moist dough.
- Transfer to non-reactive container; cover loosely, permitting gas to escape.
- Ferment 6~8 hours at cool room temp until roughly double in bulk.

Bread

1½ C	354 g	Warm Water (120°~130°F)
1 TBS	12 g	Sugar
2 C	240 g	Bread Flour
1 TBS	10 g	Instant Yeast
1 TBS	10 g	Salt (DC kosher)
Preferment	(all)	From Day Before
2 C	240 g	All-Purpose Flour
2 TBS	21 g	Semolina or flour for pan

- Measure warm water into mixer work bowl.
- Mix in sugar and bread flour to create a batter.
- With batter temperature under 110°F, mix in yeast.
- Let batter rest for 15~30 minutes (autolyse) while sponge develops.
- Mix salt and preferment into batter, approximately a quarter at a time.
- Mix in 1¾ C of all-purpose flour, half at a time, on low~medium speed.
- Dust dough and counter with ¼ C flour and turn out.
- Stretch and fold to knead, using a bench scraper initially as required.
- Rise, covered, until doubled in bulk.
- Preheat oven (and baking stone if available) to 450°F while dough rises.
- Dust round cake pans with semolina or flour; do not use cornmeal.
- Gently release dough from bowl with rubber spatula; divide in half.
- Fold dough on itself to tighten and shape into boules (round ball).
- Put shaped loaves into prepared pans.
- Allow loaves to rise until not quite double, about 20 minutes.
- Dust loaves with flour if desired and slash in a windowpane pattern.
- Bake to golden brown and a tap on the bottom sounds hollow, ~ 30 minutes.
- Mist oven with water several times during the first 10 minutes.
- Cool on a wire rack before cutting or storing.

DIMPLED ROLLS
French & Belgian Style

1 C	244 g	Milk
1 C	236 g	Water
1 TBS	12 g	Sugar
2¾ C	330 g	Bread Flour
1 TBS	10 g	Instant Yeast
1 TBS	10 g	Salt (DC kosher)
2¼ C	270 g	All-Purpose Flour (approx)
2 TBS	21 g	Semolina or flour for pan

- Combine water and milk and warm to 120°~130°F.
- Transfer warm liquids into a large mixing bowl.
- Mix in sugar and bread flour to create a batter.
- With batter temperature under 110°F, mix in yeast.
- Let batter rest for 15~30 minutes (autolyse) while sponge develops.
- Mix salt into batter.
- Beat in 2 C of A-P flour, 1 C at a time; mix until well incorporated.
- Mix in additional flour, 2 TBS at a time, until dough starts to release from bowl.
- Dust dough and counter lightly with flour and turn dough out.
- Knead until dough is smooth and elastic, adding flour only as necessary.
- Shape dough into a tight ball.
- Rise, covered, in a lightly oiled bowl until doubled in bulk.
- Preheat oven to 450°F while the dough rises.
- Prepare sheet pan with parchment (optional); sprinkle pan with semolina.
- Fold dough on itself a few times and knead briefly.
- Divide dough in half and then divide each half into 8 pieces.
- Shape each piece into a smooth elongated ball.
- Dust the tops lightly with flour before creasing.
- Using a wooden spoon's handle, press a deep crease in the top of each piece.
- Place shaped and creased rolls on the prepared pan.
- Allow rolls to rise, covered, until not quite double, about 20 minutes.
- Bake to golden and done, about 15 minutes.
- Mist oven with water twice during the first 5~7 minutes.
- Enjoy warm or cool on a wire rack before storing.

> **Recipe Tips**
> When dimpling these rolls, don't go all the way through, just far enough to make a deep crease. Widen the crease slightly so it remains after rising.

PETIT PAINS AU LAIT
French Milk Rolls

1½ C	366 g	Warm Milk (120°-130°F)
¼ C	50 g	Sugar
2 C	240 g	Bread Flour
1 TBS	10 g	Instant Yeast
1 TBS	10 g	Salt (DC kosher)
6 TBS	85 g	Butter, softened (¾ stick)
2¼ C	270 g	All-Purpose Flour (approx)
2 TBS	21 g	Semolina or flour for pan
2 TBS	30 g	Milk for glazing

- Warm milk and transfer into a large mixing bowl.
- Mix in sugar and 2 C of bread flour to create a batter.
- With batter temperature under 110°F, mix in yeast.
- Let batter rest for 15~30 minutes (autolyse) while sponge develops.
- Mix salt and butter into batter, approximately 1 TBS at a time.
- Beat in 2 C of A-P flour, 1 C at a time; mix until well incorporated.
- Mix in additional flour, 2 TBS at a time, until dough starts to release from bowl.
- Dust dough and counter lightly with flour and turn dough out.
- Knead until dough is smooth and elastic, adding flour only as necessary.
- Shape dough into a tight ball.
- Rise, covered, in a lightly oiled bowl until doubled in bulk.
- Preheat oven to 375°F while the dough rises.
- Prepare sheet pan with parchment (optional); sprinkle pan with semolina.
- Fold dough on itself a few times and knead briefly.
- Divide dough in half and then divide each half into 8 pieces.
- Shape each piece into a smooth ball and place on prepared pan.
- Cut a cross in the top of each ball using sharp scissors or a serrated knife.
- Use 3 cuts: one across the top, then cut the first cut in half on each side.
- Allow rolls to rise, covered, until not quite double, about 20 minutes.
- Brush rolls with milk just before baking.
- Bake to golden and just done, about 15~18 minutes; do not over-bake.
- Enjoy warm or cool on a wire rack before storing.

Recipe Tip
- To make into long rolls, divide each half into 4~6 pieces. First shape into round balls, then roll back and forth forming rolls 4~5 inches long with tapered ends. Slash the tops 2~3 times before baking.

PAIN D'EPI
French Wheat Stalk Bread

1 C	275 g	Mother Starter
1 C	236 g	Hot Water (180°F)
2 tsp	6 g	Instant Yeast
2 tsp	6 g	Salt (DC kosher)
3 C	360 g	All-Purpose Flour
1 TBS	11 g	Semolina for pan

- Bring starter to room temperature in a large mixing bowl.
- Mix hot water into starter.
- Mix in 1 C of flour to make a batter.
- With batter temperature under 110°F, mix in yeast.
- Let batter rest for 15~30 minutes (autolyse) while sponge develops.
- Mix in salt.
- Beat in 1½ C of additional flour, ½ C at a time.
- Dust dough and counter with ¼ C of flour (reserve ¼ C).
- Turn dough out onto counter.
- Stretch and fold to knead; dough should be sticky inside; do not over flour.
- Rise, covered, in a warm place until doubled in bulk.
- Preheat oven (and baking stone if available) to 475°F while dough rises.
- Divide dough in half (for two 1# batches). Do not punch down; be gentle!
- Prepare sheet pan with parchment (optional); sprinkle pan with semolina.
- Shape by folding, sealing, and rolling into a demi-baguette.
- Transfer shaped dough to prepared pan.
- Allow dough to rise until almost but not quite doubled.
- When the dough has risen, dust the loaf lightly with flour.
- Just before baking, cut dough with scissors at 30° angle to shape the epi.
- Cut nearly through at 2½-inch intervals and move sections to alternating sides.
- Bake to golden color and done ~25 minutes.
- Cool on a wire rack before breaking into rolls or storing.

BAGUETTES
Classic French Loaves

Poolish Preferment
1 C	236 g	Room Temperature Water (75°F)
2 C	240 g	Bread Flour (can include 2~3 TBS Whole Wheat)
¼ tsp	¾ g	Instant Yeast

- Mix ingredients well in a non-reactive container.
- Cover loosely, permitting gas to escape.
- Ferment at room temp 6~8 hours until triple in bulk.

Bread
Preferment	(all)	from recipe above
1 C	236 g	Very Hot Water (200°F)
1½ C	180 g	Bread Flour
1 TBS	10 g	Instant Yeast
1 TBS	10 g	Salt (DC kosher)
2 C	240 g	All-Purpose Flour
2 TBS	21 g	Semolina for pan

- Transfer preferment into a large mixing bowl.
- Mix in hot water and bread flour to create a batter.
- With batter temperature under 110°F, mix in yeast.
- Let batter rest for 15~30 minutes (autolyse) while sponge develops.
- Mix in salt; then mix in 1¾ C of all-purpose flour, half at a time.
- Dust dough and counter with remaining ¼ C flour and turn out.
- Stretch and fold to knead, using a bench scraper initially as required.
- Rise, covered, until doubled in bulk.
- Preheat oven (and baking stone if available) to 475°F while dough rises.
- Prepare sheet pan with parchment (optional); sprinkle pan with semolina.
- Gently release dough from bowl with rubber spatula.
- Fold dough on itself a few times to tighten and divide in half.
- Divide each half into 2 or 3 pieces and shape into baguettes as follows.
- Flatten dough, fold in half, seal seam, and roll to form each baguette.
- Put shaped loaves between folds of a well-floured couche or lint-free towel.
- Dust loaves lightly with flour, cover, and let rise until not quite double.
- Using a long thin board, gently transfer risen loaves to prepared pan.
- Slash each loaf several times in a long diagonal pattern.
- Bake to golden and done, about 20~25 minutes.
- Mist oven with water several times during the first 5~7 minutes.
- Cool on a wire rack before cutting or storing.

CRUMPETS
English Muffins

1 C	244 g	Milk, warmed to 120°F
2 tsp	8 g	Sugar
2 tsp	6 g	Instant Yeast
2 tsp	6 g	Salt (DC kosher)
1 tsp	5 g	Baking Powder
2⅔ C	320 g	All-Purpose Flour (approx)
¼ C	42 g	Cornmeal or Semolina for bench

- Warm milk in a saucepan or microwave.
- Stir sugar into milk to dissolve.
- Pour sweetened milk into a mixing bowl.
- Mix in 1½ C of flour; beat well.
- With batter temperature under 110°F, mix in yeast.
- Optionally, let batter rest 15~30 minutes (autolyse) while sponge develops.
- Mix in salt and baking powder and then 1 additional C of flour.
- Mix in more flour, ¼ C at a time, until dough starts to release from bowl.
- Dust dough and counter lightly with flour and turn dough out.
- Knead briefly; adding only enough flour to prevent sticking.
- Rise, covered, in a lightly oiled bowl until doubled in bulk.
- Preheat griddle or electric skillet to 275°F while dough rises.
- Prepare work surface with a sprinkle of cornmeal or semolina.
- Fold dough on itself a few times and knead briefly.
- Roll dough out to ~ ½-inch thick.
- Cut into rounds and place on an ungreased baking sheet to rise.
- When puffy, bake on griddle to golden brown and just done, ~ 10 minutes/side.
- Cool on a wire rack before cutting or storing.

> **Recipe Tip**
>
> For fresh muffins on a hot summer day, try baking these on a griddle or heavy sheet pan on top of the grill. You won't heat up the kitchen, and they make nice burger buns too!

ENGLISH DINNER ROLLS
with assorted toppings

1½ C	354 g	Warm Water (120°~130°F)
⅓ C	23 g	Instant Dry Milk
2 TBS	25 g	Sugar
1 TBS	10 g	Instant Yeast
1 TBS	10 g	Salt (DC kosher)
4 TBS	57 g	Butter, softened (½ stick)
1 large	19 g	Egg Yolk, beaten (reserve white)
5 C	600 g	All-Purpose Flour (approx)
2 TBS	21 g	Semolina
1 large	30 g	Egg White, beaten with 1 tsp Water
1 TBS	10 g	Poppy or Sesame Seeds (optional)

- Measure warm water into a large mixing bowl.
- Mix in milk, sugar, and 2 C of flour; stir briskly until smooth.
- With batter temperature under 110°F, mix in yeast.
- Optionally, let batter rest 15~30 minutes (autolyse) while sponge develops.
- Mix in salt, butter, and egg yolk.
- Mix in 2 C of flour, one at a time.
- Mix in additional flour, ¼ C at a time, until dough starts to release from bowl.
- Dust dough and counter lightly with flour and turn dough out.
- Knead until dough is smooth and elastic, adding flour only as necessary.
- Shape dough into a tight ball.
- Rise, covered, in a lightly oiled bowl until doubled in bulk.
- Prepare sheet pan with parchment (optional); sprinkle pan with semolina.
- Fold risen dough on itself a few times and knead briefly to de-gas.
- Using bench scraper, divide dough into 12 equal pieces.
- Shape each piece as desired and place rolls on prepared pan.
- Space rolls about an inch apart so they won't rise into each other.
- Allow rolls to rise, covered, until not quite double, about 20~30 minutes.
- Preheat oven to 400°F while the dough rises.
- Brush with egg wash and sprinkle with seeds as desired.
- Bake 15~18 minutes until golden and just done; do not over-bake.
- Enjoy warm or cool on a wire rack before storing.

INTERNATIONAL

> Recipe Tip
> For a softer crust brush with butter instead of an egg wash.

CHEESE AND ONION BREAD

1½ C	250 g	Sweet Onion, finely chopped
2 TBS	28 g	Butter
2 C	472 g	Warm Water (120°~130°F)
⅓ C	23 g	Instant Dry Milk
1 TBS	10 g	Instant Yeast
1 TBS	10 g	Salt (DC kosher)
2 tsp	6 g	Dry Mustard
½ tsp	1 g	Ground Black Pepper
3 C	339 g	Cheddar Cheese, grated
6 C	720 g	Bread Flour

- Saute onion in butter until soft and translucent; set aside to cool.
- Measure warm water into a large mixing bowl.
- Mix in milk and 3 C flour; stir briskly until smooth.
- With batter temperature under 110°F, mix in yeast.
- Optionally, let batter rest 15~30 minutes (autolyse) while sponge develops.
- Mix in salt, mustard, pepper, cooked onion, and 2 C cheese (reserve 1 C).
- Mix in 2 C flour, one at a time.
- Mix in additional flour, ¼ C at a time, until dough starts to release from bowl.
- Dust dough and counter lightly with flour and turn dough out.
- Knead until dough is smooth and elastic, adding flour only as necessary.
- Rise, covered, in a lightly oiled bowl until doubled in bulk.
- Prepare 2 loaf pans: parchment on bottom, spray sides with release (PAM).
- Release risen dough from bowl with rubber spatula; divide in half.
- Fold dough on itself several times to tighten and shape into loaves.
- Put shaped loaves into prepared pans.
- Allow loaves to rise until not quite double, about 20 minutes.
- Preheat oven to 375°F while bread rises.
- Divide and sprinkle remaining cheese on tops of risen loaves.
- Bake 45 ~ 50 minutes until golden brown.
- Tent with foil halfway through baking when tops are golden.
- Cool on a wire rack before cutting or storing.

> **Recipe Tip**
> - Try adding 2~3 TBS of chopped or diced cooked bacon. If you do you should also cut some of the salt in the recipe.

SAFFRON CAKE
Traditional Cornish Recipe

1½ C	354 g	Boiling Hot Water (210°F)
½ tsp	0.25 g	Saffron (¼ tsp crushed)
¾ C	120 g	Dried Fruit (raisins, currents, cranberries, etc)
¼ C	17 g	Instant Dry Milk (optional)
¼ C	50 g	Sugar
½ C	113 g	Butter, softened
2 large	100 g	Eggs, beaten
2½ C	300 g	Bread Flour
1 TBS	10 g	Instant Yeast
1 tsp	3 g	Cinnamon
½ tsp	1 g	Nutmeg
1 TBS	10 g	Salt (DC kosher)
1 TBS	6 g	Zest of 1 Lemon (optional)
3 C	360 g	All-purpose Flour

- Warm eggs in hot tap water while you continue with the recipe.
- Crush saffron with mortar and pestle; transfer to mixing bowl.
- Pour hot water over saffron; steep 5 minutes.
- Add fruit to hot water; plump for 5 minutes.
- Mix in milk, sugar, butter, beaten eggs, and bread flour.
- With batter temperature under 110°F, mix in yeast.
- Let batter rest for 15~30 minutes (autolyse) while sponge develops.
- Mix in spices, salt, and lemon.
- Mix in 2 C of A-P flour 1 C at a time.
- Mix in additional A-P flour ¼ C at a time until dough just releases from bowl.
- Dust dough and counter with flour and turn out.
- Stretch and fold to knead, using a bench scraper as required.
- Rise, covered, until doubled in bulk.
- Preheat oven to 375°F while dough rises.
- Lightly grease two 8½ x 4½-inch loaf pans.
- Gently release dough from bowl with rubber spatula; divide in half.
- Fold dough on itself to tighten and shape into loaves.
- Put shaped loaves into prepared pans.
- Allow loaves to rise until not quite double, about 20 minutes.
- Bake to golden brown and hollow sound when tapped, about 35 minutes.
- Cool on a wire rack before cutting or storing.

CHELSEA BUNS

Dough

1½ C	366 g	Milk, scalded
⅓ C	67 g	Sugar
¼ C	57 g	Butter, softened (½ stick)
1 large	50 g	Egg, beaten
1 TBS	10 g	Instant Yeast
1 TBS	10 g	Salt (DC kosher)
5 C	600 g	All-purpose Flour (approx)

Filling

¼ C	57 g	Butter, melted (½ stick)
½ C	100 g	Sugar, fine granulated
1½ C	240 g	Dried Fruit (raisins, currents, cranberries, etc)

Icing

3 TBS	45 g	Milk (approx)
2 packets	2 g	True Orange (or ½ tsp extract)
1 tsp	5 g	Corn Syrup
1 C	115 g	Confectioners Sugar

Recipe Tips

This icing is unique in that it "sets up". Wait until the buns are cool before applying.

- Scald milk in saucepan or microwave to 180°F; transfer to large mixing bowl.
- Mix in sugar and butter; then mix in beaten egg and 2½ C flour.
- With batter temperature under 110°F, mix in yeast.
- Optionally, let batter rest 15~30 minutes (autolyse) while sponge develops.
- Mix in salt; then mix in 2 C flour, one at a time.
- Mix in additional flour, ¼ C at a time, until dough releases from bowl.
- Dust dough and counter with flour, turn out, and knead until smooth.
- Rise, covered, in a lightly oiled bowl until doubled in bulk.
- Prepare 2 sheet pans with parchment while dough rises.
- Fold risen dough on itself a few times; knead briefly; divide in half.
- Roll out each half to a rectangle 18 inches wide x 12 inches deep.
- Brush each dough with 2 TBS melted butter.
- Sprinkle each dough with ¼ C sugar and half of the fruit.
- From long side, roll up toward you into a log as for a jelly roll.
- Cut log into slices ~ 1 inch thick.
- Place rolls on prepared pan in pairs with tails touching to prevent unwinding.
- Allow rolls to rise until almost but not quite double.
- Preheat oven to 375°F while dough rises.
- Bake risen rolls 18~20 minutes until golden and just done.
- Cool on a wire rack before drizzling with icing.

based on recipe & techniques by Michael Jubinsky

LARDY CAKE
Traditional Southern (English) Recipe

Dough
1½ C	354 g	Warm Water (120°~130°F)
2 TBS	25 g	Sugar
1 TBS	10 g	Instant Yeast
1 TBS	10 g	Salt (DC kosher)
1 TBS	14 g	Butter (softened) or Lard
4 C	480 g	Bread Flour

Filling (divided)
6 TBS	77 g	Lard, cut into flakes
6 TBS	82 g	Light Brown Sugar
1 C	160 g	Dried Fruit (raisins, currents, cranberries, etc)
1 tsp	3 g	Allspice

Topping
1 TBS	14 g	Butter (melted) or Oil
2 TBS	25 g	Sugar

> **Recipe Tip**
> Lard has less saturated fat and twice the monounsaturated fat compared to butter.

- Measure warm water into a large mixing bowl.
- Mix in sugar and then 2 C flour to create a batter.
- With batter temperature under 110°F, mix in yeast.
- Let batter rest for 15~30 minutes (autolyse) while sponge develops.
- Mix in salt, butter/lard, and 1½ C flour, half at a time, until well incorporated.
- Mix in additional flour, ¼ C at a time, until dough starts to release from bowl.
- Dust dough and counter lightly with flour and turn out.
- Knead until dough is smooth and elastic, adding flour only as necessary.
- Rise dough, covered, in a lightly oiled bowl until doubled in bulk.
- While the dough rises, prepare an 8 x 10-inch shallow roasting pan.
- Line the bottom with parchment (cut to fit) and lightly grease the sides.
- Degas dough and turn out onto a lightly floured surface; knead briefly.
- Roll dough into a rectangle about ¼-inch thick.
- Warm fruit briefly in microwave to soften.
- Dot upper two thirds of dough with half the lard.
- Sprinkle this part of dough with half the brown sugar, allspice, and fruit.
- Fold uncoated bottom third up and then fold again like a letter; seal edges.
- Turn dough 90° and repeat, rolling and covering with remaining toppings.
- Seal edges and roll to fit prepared pan; transfer to pan.
- Rise dough, covered with lightly-oiled wrap, until almost doubled.
- Preheat oven to 400°F while dough rises.
- Brush top with melted butter or oil and sprinkle with 1~2 TBS sugar.
- Score top in a criss-cross pattern and bake to golden, 30~35 minutes.
- Cool briefly and serve warm, cut into either slices or squares.

MALTED CURRANT BREAD

1½ C	366 g	Milk, scalded
1 C	160 g	Currants
½ C	113 g	Butter (1 stick)
⅓ C	112 g	Malt Extract
¼ C	84 g	Golden Syrup
2½ C	300 g	Bread Flour
1 TBS	10 g	Instant Yeast
2 tsp	6 g	Allspice
1 TBS	10 g	DC Kosher Salt
3 C	360 g	All-Purpose Flour (approx)
1 TBS	15 g	Milk for glaze
1 TBS	12 g	Sugar for glaze

Recipe Tip
Use Lyle's Golden Syrup or equal for authentic flavor.

- Scald milk in saucepan or microwave to 180°F.
- Plump currants in hot milk 1~2 minutes.
- Add butter; stir to melt; mix in extract and syrup; re-heat to 130°F.
- Transfer warm milk mixture to K-A mixer work bowl.
- Using paddle attachment (not dough hook), mix in bread flour.
- With batter temperature under 110°F, mix in yeast.
- Optionally, let batter rest 15~30 minutes (autolyse) while sponge develops.
- Mix in spice, salt and 2 C of all-purpose flour.
- Mix in more A-P flour, ¼ C at a time, until dough starts to release from bowl.
- Dust dough and counter lightly with flour and turn dough out.
- Knead dough briefly and shape into a smooth ball.
- Rise dough, covered, in a lightly oiled bowl until doubled in bulk.
- Lightly butter the sides of 2 loaf pans.
- Line the bottoms of the pans with parchment cut to fit.
- Fold dough on itself a few times; divide in half.
- Shape into loaves; place in prepared pans.
- Allow dough to rise, covered, until almost but not quite doubled.
- Preheat oven to 350°F while dough rises.
- Bake loaves 35~40 minutes until done.
- Mix glaze while breads bake: 1 TBS sugar dissolved in 1 TBS milk.
- Tent tops with foil if they appear to be browning too rapidly.
- Remove loaves from pans to a wire rack.
- Brush with glaze while still hot.
- Cool before cutting or storing.

SPOTTED DOG
Irish Soda Bread

1 C	160 g	Raisins
2 tsp	6 g	Caraway Seeds (optional)
1 TBS	14 g	Irish Whiskey (warmed)
4 C	480 g	All-Purpose Flour
3 TBS	38 g	Sugar
1 tsp	3 g	Salt (DC kosher)
1 TBS	14 g	Baking Powder
1 tsp	5 g	Baking Soda
2 large	100 g	Eggs
4 TBS	55 g	Oil (or melted butter/margarine)
1½ C	368 g	Buttermilk or Sour Milk

- Preheat oven to 400°F while you proceed with the recipe.
- In a small bowl, toss raisins and caraway seeds with whiskey.
- Line the sides and bottom of a round casserole or pan with parchment.
- Measure flour into a large mixing bowl.
- Mix sugar, salt, baking powder and soda into flour.
- Stir raisins and caraway seeds into flour mixture.
- In a small bowl, beat the eggs.
- Whisk oil and buttermilk with eggs; add drained whiskey if desired.
- Gradually add wet ingredients to dry until dough is firm but not stiff.
- Be careful to not add more wet ingredients than necessary!
- If you do, and the dough becomes too wet, you will need to add more flour.
- Turn dough out onto floured surface; knead briefly (less than 1 minute).
- Shape dough into a ball and place in the prepared casserole.
- With a sharp knife cut a cross 1 inch deep in top of dough.
- Bake about 40~50 minutes until cake tester comes out clean.
- Remove from casserole; cool on a wire rack before cutting or storing.

Recipe Tip
To make sour milk (substitute for buttermilk):
Put 3 TBS lemon juice in a measuring cup;
Add milk to make 1½ C total and stir.

SCOTTISH MORNING ROLLS

1½ C	354 g	Warm Water (120°~130°F)
⅓ C	23 g	Instant Dry Milk
1 TBS	10 g	Instant Yeast
1 TBS	10 g	Salt (DC kosher)
4 C	480 g	All-Purpose Flour (approx)
2 TBS	21 g	Semolina

> **Recipe Tip**
> When pressing these rolls, don't go all the way through, just far enough to equalize the pressure.

- Measure warm water into a large mixing bowl.
- Mix in milk and then 2 C flour to create a batter.
- With batter temperature under 110°F, mix in yeast.
- Let batter rest for 15~30 minutes (autolyse) while sponge develops.
- Mix in salt and then 1½ C flour, half at a time, until well incorporated.
- Mix in additional flour, ¼ C at a time, until dough starts to release from bowl.
- Dust dough and counter lightly with flour and turn dough out.
- Knead until dough is smooth and elastic, adding flour only as necessary.
- Rise dough, covered, in a lightly oiled bowl until doubled in bulk.
- Prepare sheet pan with parchment (optional); sprinkle pan with semolina.
- Fold dough on itself a few times and knead briefly to de-gas.
- Divide dough into 10 equal size pieces (about 85 g each).
- Shape each piece into a flat 3x4-inch oval or 3½-inch round.
- Place rolls on the prepared pan.
- Allow rolls to rise, covered, until not quite double, about 20 minutes.
- Preheat oven to 400°F while the dough rises.
- Press each roll lightly in center with 3 fingers to even surface.
- Brush rolls with milk and dust with coarse flour.
- Bake to golden and done, about 15 minutes.
- Enjoy warm or cool on a wire rack before storing.

CLASSIC CURRANT SCONES
Scottish Quick Bread

1½ C	180 g	All-Purpose Flour
½ C	52 g	Oatmeal Flour
2 TBS	25 g	Sugar (white or brown)
½ tsp	2 g	Salt (DC kosher)
2 tsp	9 g	Baking Powder
½ tsp	3 g	Baking Soda
5 TBS	75 g	Butter, frozen (⅓ C)
½ C	80 g	Currants
½ tsp	2 g	Ground Cinnamon
1 C	244 g	Buttermilk or Sour Milk (approx)

> **Recipe Tip**
> To make sour milk (substitute for buttermilk): Put 2 TBS lemon juice in a measuring cup; Add milk to make 1 C total and stir.

- Preheat oven to 400°F while you proceed with the recipe.
- Prepare sheet pan with parchment or light coating of grease.
- Sift flours, sugar, salt, baking powder and soda into a mixing bowl.
- Grate butter into flour mixture.
- Add currants and cinnamon.
- Add milk as required to moisten and mix to form a ball.
- Be careful to not add more milk than necessary!
- Knead gently on floured surface 5~10 times (less than 1 minute).
- Pat dough to a form a ½-inch thick round disk.
- Cut round into 6~8 pie shaped wedges.
- Place wedges on prepared pan.
- Bake 18~20 minutes until golden and just done (test with toothpick).
- Enjoy warm or cool completely before storing.

INTERNATIONAL

BAUERNBROT
German Farmer's Bread

1½ C	366 g	Milk
3 TBS	30 g	Vinegar (optional)
1 C	228 g	Plain Yogurt
4 tsp	12 g	Instant Yeast
4 tsp	12 g	Salt (DC kosher)
1 TBS	9 g	Caraway Seeds
½ C	39 g	Rolled Oats
1½ C	180 g	Rye Flour
1½ C	180 g	Whole Wheat Flour
3 C	360 g	Bread Flour (approx)
1 TBS	11 g	Semolina for dusting pans

- Measure milk into a saucepan.
- Stir in vinegar to make sour milk.
- Mix in yogurt.
- Heat gently, stirring continuously, to warm (120°~130°F).
- Transfer liquids to a large mixing bowl.
- Mix in 2 C bread flour; beat well.
- With batter temperature under 110°F, mix in yeast.
- Optionally, let batter rest 15~30 minutes (autolyse) while sponge develops.
- Mix in salt and seeds (if desired).
- Beat in oats, rye flour, and whole wheat flour, one at a time.
- Dust dough and counter lightly with flour and turn dough out.
- Knead until dough is smooth and elastic, adding flour only as necessary.
- Rise, covered, in a lightly oiled bowl until doubled in bulk.
- Preheat oven to 450°F while dough rises.
- Prepare sheet pan with parchment (optional); sprinkle pan with semolina.
- Divide dough in half.
- Shape into round loaves and place on prepared pan.
- Rise, covered, until almost but not quite doubled. Do not allow to over-rise!
- Dust loaves lightly with flour and slash about ¼-inch deep just before baking.
- Bake 20 minutes at 450°F.
- Lower oven temp to 350°F and bake another 20 minutes until done.
- Cool on a wire rack before cutting or storing.

Recipe Tips
You can also make these loaves in 8-inch oven-proof skillets. To prep, spray lightly with release (PAM) and sprinkle with semolina.

STOLLEN
German Christmas Bread

1½ C	366 g	Milk, scalded
1 C	160 g	Raisins and/or Currants
½ C	113 g	Butter/Margarine (1 stick)
½ C	100 g	Sugar
½ tsp	1 g	Cardamom, ground
1 tsp	2 g	Cinnamon, ground
2 tsp	8 g	Vanilla Extract
2 large	100 g	Eggs, beaten
4 tsp	13 g	Instant Yeast
4 tsp	13 g	Salt (DC kosher)
½ C	73 g	Almonds, chopped or slivered
¼ Can	89 g	Almond Pastry Filling
6½ C	780 g	All-Purpose Flour (approx)

- Warm eggs in hot tap water while you continue.
- Scald milk in saucepan or microwave to 180°F; add raisins to hot milk to plump.
- Add butter/margarine to hot milk to melt.
- Dissolve sugar in milk mixture; then mix in spices and vanilla.
- In a large bowl, beat eggs; add milk mixture to beaten eggs.
- Mix in 3 C of flour; beat well by hand or with mixer.
- With batter temperature under 110°F, mix in yeast.
- Optionally, let batter rest 15~30 minutes (autolyse) while sponge develops.
- Mix in salt, almonds, and then 3 additional C of flour, one cup at a time.
- Mix in more flour, ¼ C at a time, until dough starts to release from bowl.
- Dust dough and counter lightly with flour and turn dough out.
- Knead until dough is smooth and elastic, adding flour only as necessary.
- Rise, covered, in a lightly oiled bowl until doubled in bulk.
- Line a sheet pan with parchment.
- Fold dough on itself a few times; knead briefly; divide in half.
- Shape dough into rounds, flatten, and roll out to a rectangle ¾-inch thick.
- Spread almond filling over center of rectangle leaving a 2-inch border.
- Fold dough in thirds (like a letter) with the top edge slightly in from the bottom.
- Transfer loaves to prepared pan and cover with plastic wrap.
- Allow dough to rise until almost but not quite doubled.
- Preheat oven to 400°F while dough rises.
- Bake 30~35 minutes until golden and done.
- Tent loaves with foil if they appear to be browning too rapidly.
- Remove baked loaves from oven and brush with melted butter.
- Cool on a wire rack before cutting or storing.
- Dust cooled loaves with confectioners' sugar just before serving.

BABKA
Updated Authentic Polish Recipe

1¾ C	427 g	Milk, scalded
1 C	160 g	Raisins (golden preferred)
½ C	113 g	Butter/Margarine (1 stick)
⅔ C	133 g	Sugar
1 TBS	14 g	Vanilla Extract
5 large	95 g	Egg Yolks, beaten
4 tsp	13 g	Instant Yeast
½ C	72 g	Candied Peel (optional)
4 tsp	13 g	Salt (DC kosher)
6¾ C	810 g	All-Purpose Flour (approx)

Recipe Tip
Egg whites can make bread dry so this recipe leaves them out.

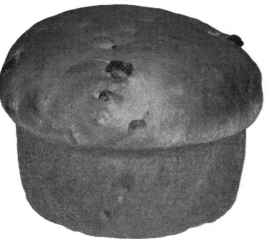

- Warm eggs in hot tap water while you continue.
- Scald milk in saucepan or microwave to 180°F.
- Add raisins to hot milk to plump.
- Add butter/margarine to hot milk to melt.
- Dissolve sugar in milk mixture; then add vanilla.
- In a large bowl, beat egg yolks.
- Add milk mixture to beaten egg yolks.
- Mix in 3 C of flour; beat well by hand or with mixer.
- With batter temperature under 110°F, mix in yeast.
- Optionally, let batter rest 15~30 minutes (autolyse) while sponge develops.
- Mix in candied peel if desired.
- Mix in salt and then 3 additional C of flour, one cup at a time.
- Mix in more flour, ¼ C at a time, until dough starts to release from bowl.
- Dust dough and counter lightly with flour and turn dough out.
- Knead until dough is smooth and elastic, adding flour only as necessary.
- Rise, covered, in a lightly oiled bowl until doubled in bulk.
- Lightly grease the sides of 2 round casseroles.
- Line the bottom of the casseroles with parchment cut to fit.
- Fold dough on itself a few times; knead briefly; divide in half.
- Shape dough into rounds; place into prepared casseroles.
- Allow dough to rise, covered, until almost but not quite doubled.
- Preheat oven to 250°F while dough rises.
- Option: for a shiny crust brush tops with an egg wash before baking.
- Bake at 250°F for 10 minutes.
- Raise temp to 350°F and bake 35~45 additional minutes until golden.
- Tent tops with foil if they appear to be browning too rapidly.
- Remove from casseroles; cool on a wire rack before cutting or storing.

BIALYS
Polish Bialystok Kuchen

Dough
2 C	472 g	Warm Water (120°~130°F)
1 TBS	13 g	Granulated Sugar
2 C	240 g	Bread Flour
1 TBS	10 g	Instant Yeast
1 TBS	10 g	Salt (DC kosher)
3¼ C	390 g	All-Purpose Flour (approx)

Topping
1 TBS	14 g	Olive Oil
2 tsp	6 g	Poppy Seeds
⅓ C	50 g	Onion, minced
½ tsp	1½ g	Salt (DC kosher)

- Measure warm water into a large mixing bowl.
- Mix in sugar and bread flour; stir briskly until smooth.
- With batter temperature under 110°F, mix in yeast.
- Optionally, let batter rest 15~30 minutes (autolyse) while sponge develops.
- Mix in salt and then 2 C of A/P flour, one at a time.
- Mix in additional A/P flour, ¼ C at a time, until dough starts to release from bowl.
- Dust dough and counter lightly with flour and turn dough out.
- Knead until dough is smooth and elastic, adding flour only as necessary.
- Rise, covered, in a lightly oiled bowl until doubled in bulk.
- Mix filling while dough rises.
- Prepare 2 sheet pans with parchment and sprinkle with semolina.
- Fold risen dough on itself a few times; knead briefly.
- Divide dough into 8 equal size pieces; bench rest 5~10 minutes.
- On a floured surface, pat pieces into rounds 3~4 inches in diameter.
- Do not pat out more rounds than you can bake at one time.
- Place rounds on prepared parchment.
- Let rolls rise, covered, until only half-doubled in size.
- Preheat oven to 425°F while rolls rise.
- Make an indentation in the center of each roll leaving a 1-inch rim.
- Put 1 tsp of onion filling in the center depression.
- Dust lightly with flour and allow to rise, covered, an additional 15 minutes.
- Bake 11 ~ 13 minutes until lightly browned; to keep soft, do not overbake.
- Repeat steps to bake the rest of the dough.
- Enjoy warm or cool on a wire rack before storing.

MULTIGRAIN POLARBRØD
Swedish Mjukkaka

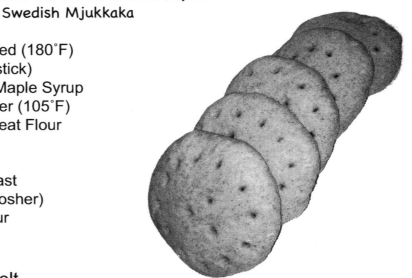

1 C	244 g	Milk, scalded (180°F)
4 TBS	57 g	Butter (½ stick)
2 TBS	39 g	Honey or Maple Syrup
1 C	236 g	Warm Water (105°F)
1¼ C	150 g	Whole Wheat Flour
¾ C	90 g	Rye Flour
¾ C	78 g	Oat Flour
2¼ tsp	7 g	Instant Yeast
2 tsp	7 g	Salt (DC kosher)
2½ C	300 g	Bread Flour

- Scald milk to 180°F.
- Add butter to hot milk; stir to melt.
- Mix in honey, water, whole wheat, rye, and oats; stir briskly until smooth.
- With batter temperature under 110°F, mix in yeast.
- Optionally, let batter rest 15~30 minutes (autolyse) while sponge develops.
- Mix salt into batter; then mix in 2 C bread flour, one at a time.
- Mix in more bread flour until dough starts to release from bowl.
- Dust dough and counter lightly with flour and turn dough out.
- Knead until dough is smooth and elastic, adding flour only as necessary.
- Rise, covered, in a lightly oiled bowl until doubled in bulk.
- Preheat oven to 500°F while dough rises.
- Place an inverted sheet pan (or baking stone) in the oven to preheat.
- Ready 2 sheet pan size pieces of parchment; optionally dust with semolina.
- Fold dough on itself a few times; knead briefly; divide in half.
- Roll dough out into a rope; cut rope into 8 equal size (~ 75 g) pieces.
- Shape pieces into smooth balls; then roll into circles ~ ½ inch thick.
- Place 4 pieces on each sheet of prepared parchment.
- Use a chopstick to "dock" (prick) a dozen or more holes in each piece.
- Cover the dough with plastic wrap and rest for ~ 15 minutes.
- While first batch rests, roll and shape the other half of dough.
- Transfer parchment with rested dough to the oven; bake ~ 4 minutes.
- Breads will be slightly puffed up and light brown on top when done.
- Repeat the process to shape, dock, rest, and bake remaining breads.
- Enjoy breads warm or cool completely before storing in the freezer.

Recipe Tip
Use a food processor to convert rolled oats into flour for this recipe:
1 C rolled oats makes ¾ C oat flour

PULLA
Finnish Cardamom Braid

1½ C	366 g	Milk, scalded
½ C	113 g	Butter/Margarine (1 stick)
½ C	100 g	Sugar
1 TBS	10 g	Instant Yeast
1 TBS	10 g	Salt (DC kosher)
1 large	50 g	Eggs, beaten
1 large	19 g	Egg Yolk (reserve white)
1 tsp	4 g	Cardamom (freshly ground)
6 C	720 g	All-Purpose Flour (approx)
Egg wash		Egg White beaten with 1 TBS Water
½ C	73 g	Almonds, sliced

- Warm 2 eggs in hot tap water while you continue.
- Scald milk in saucepan or microwave to 180°F.
- Remove coagulated proteins from top, if any.
- Measure milk into a large bowl.
- Add butter in TBS pieces; stir to melt.
- Mix in sugar; then mix in 3 C of flour; stir briskly until smooth.
- With batter temperature under 110°F, mix in yeast.
- Optionally, let batter rest 15~30 minutes (autolyse) while sponge develops.
- Separate eggs, reserving one white to make the egg wash later.
- Mix egg and yolk, salt and cardamom into batter; then mix in 3 C of flour.
- Mix in additional flour until dough starts to release from bowl.
- Dust dough and counter lightly with flour and turn dough out.
- Knead until dough is smooth and elastic, adding flour only as necessary.
- Shape dough into a smooth ball.
- Rise, covered, in a lightly oiled bowl until doubled in bulk.
- Fold dough on itself a few times and knead briefly.
- Preheat oven to 375°F while you continue with the recipe.
- Prepare a sheet pan with parchment.
- Divide dough in half; then divide each half into 3 or more equal pieces.
- Roll each piece into a 18-inch long rope; arrange in a fan for braiding.
- Braid ropes to form a loaf; optionally, pull braid into a circle/wreath.
- Place complete braid/wreath on prepared pan.
- Repeat braiding process with other ropes to create a second loaf.
- Rise, covered, until almost but not quite doubled.
- Brush with egg wash and sprinkle with almonds just before baking.
- Bake 25~30 minutes until golden and just done; do not over-bake.
- Cool on a wire rack before cutting or storing.

LIMPA
Swedish Orange Rye

1 C	248 g	Orange Juice
1 TBS	9 g	Anise/Caraway/Fennel Seeds (in any combination)
¼ C	60 g	Brown Sugar
¼ C	55 g	Oil (or melted butter/margarine)
¼ C	80 g	Molasses
1 C	236 g	Cold Water (or OJ)
4 tsp	12 g	Instant Yeast
½ tsp	1 g	Cardamom, ground
4 tsp	12 g	Salt (DC kosher)
2 TBS	12 g	Zest of 1 Orange
2 C	240 g	Rye Flour
4¼ C	510 g	Bread Flour (approx)
1 TBS	11 g	Cornmeal or Semolina for dusting pans

- Boil seeds in orange juice for 5 minutes.
- Pour hot juice with seeds into a large mixing bowl.
- Mix in sugar, oil, molasses and cold water (in that order!)
- Mix in 3 C of bread flour; beat well.
- With batter temperature under 110°F, mix in yeast.
- Optionally, let batter rest 15~30 minutes (autolyse) while sponge develops.
- Mix in cardamom, salt and orange.
- Mix in rye flour, one cup at a time.
- Mix in more bread flour, ¼ C at a time, until dough starts to release from bowl.
- Dust dough and counter lightly with bread flour and turn dough out.
- Knead until dough is smooth and elastic, adding flour only as necessary.
- Rise, covered, in a lightly oiled bowl until doubled in bulk.
- Spray pans or oven-proof skillets lightly with release (PAM).
- Sprinkle pans with cornmeal or semolina.
- Divide dough in half and shape into round loaves.
- Place loaves on prepared pans.
- Rise, covered, until almost doubled. Do not allow to over-rise!
- Preheat oven to 375°F while dough rises.
- Dust loaves lightly with flour and slash about ¼-inch deep just before baking.
- Bake 30~35 minutes until done.
- Cool on a wire rack before cutting or storing.

VORT LIMPA
Swedish Beer Bread

Bread

2 C	484 g	Dark Beer or Ale (150°F)
2 C	240 g	Rye Flour
½ C	160 g	Molasses
4 tsp	12 g	Instant Yeast
1 TBS	10 g	Salt (DC kosher)
¼ C	55 g	Oil (or melted butter)
2 TBS	12 g	Zest of 1 Orange
4⅓ C	520 g	Bread Flour (approx)
1 TBS	11 g	Semolina for dusting pans

Glaze

1 TBS	21 g	Molasses
2 TBS	30 g	Water
1 tsp	3 g	Salt (DC kosher)

- Measure and heat beer on the stove or microwave to 150°F.
- Transfer warm beer into a large mixing bowl.
- Mix in rye, molasses and 1 C of bread flour; beat well.
- With batter temperature under 110°F, mix in yeast.
- Optionally, let batter rest 15~30 minutes (autolyse) while sponge develops.
- Mix in salt, oil, and orange.
- Mix in 3 C of bread flour, one at a time.
- Mix in more bread flour, 2 TBS at a time, until dough starts to release from bowl.
- Dust dough and counter lightly with bread flour and turn dough out.
- Knead until dough is smooth and elastic, adding flour only as necessary.
- Rise, covered, in a lightly oiled bowl until doubled in bulk.
- Line the bottoms of two 2-quart non-stick pans with parchment (optional).
- Sprinkle pans with semolina; mix molasses and water for glaze.
- Divide dough in half and shape into round loaves.
- Place loaves in prepared pans.
- Rise, covered, until almost doubled. Do not allow to over-rise!
- Preheat oven to 400°F while dough rises.
- Score tops in desired pattern just before baking.
- Bake 30 minutes; then remove from pans and brush with glaze.
- Sprinkle tops with coarse salt as desired for contrast with sweet glaze.
- Reduce the temp to 350°F and bake 10~15 more minutes until done.
- Cool on a wire rack before cutting or storing.

based on techniques by Bill Egnor

RUSSIAN STYLE POTATO BREAD

2 C	472 g	Warm Water (120°~130°F)
½ C	33 g	Instant Potato Flakes
1 tsp	3 g	Caraway Seeds, crushed
1 TBS	12 g	Sugar (or Honey)
1 C	120 g	Whole Wheat Flour
1 TBS	11 g	Instant Yeast
¼ C	55 g	Oil or Butter
1 TBS	11 g	Salt (DC kosher)
3½ C	420 g	Bread Flour (approx)
1 TBS	11 g	Semolina for dusting pans

- Mix potato flakes into warm water in a large mixing bowl.
- Mix in caraway, sugar and whole wheat flour; stir briskly until smooth.
- With batter temperature under 110°F, mix in yeast.
- Optionally, let batter rest 15~30 minutes (autolyse) while sponge develops.
- Mix in oil and salt; mix in 3 C of bread flour, one at a time.
- Mix in additional flour, ¼ C at a time, until dough starts to release from bowl.
- Dust dough and counter lightly with flour and turn dough out.
- Knead until dough is smooth and elastic, adding flour only as necessary.
- Rise, covered, in a lightly oiled bowl until doubled in bulk.
- Prepare a sheet pan with parchment and sprinkle with semolina.
- Fold dough on itself a few times; knead briefly; divide in half.
- Shape into oval loaves and place on prepared baking pan.
- Rise, covered, until almost doubled.
- Preheat oven to 400°F while dough rises.
- Lightly dust tops of loaves with flour.
- Slash tops in criss-cross pattern with a sharp knife.
- Bake 30~35 minutes until done.
- Remove from pan; cool on a wire rack before cutting or storing.

> **Recipe Tips**
>
> - This bread is excellent toasted. Its open crumb is perfect for butter or jam.
>
> For real potatoes instead of flakes, use 1 C of mashed and 1¼ C of milk; mix and warm to 110°F and continue with step 2.

BLACK BREAD
Russian-style Pumpernickel

¾ C	177 g	Boiling Hot Water
1 TBS	5 g	Instant Espresso Powder (or Instant Coffee)
2 TBS	18 g	Caraway Seeds (can be crushed or ground)
1 tsp	3 g	Fennel Seeds (optional)
1 ounce	28 g	Unsweetened Chocolate (or 3 TBS Unsweetened Cocoa)
1 C	236 g	Room Temperature Water (70°F)
¼ C	55 g	Oil (or melted butter/margarine)
¼ C	80 g	Molasses (or Dark Corn Syrup)
¼ C	59 g	Cider Vinegar
4 tsp	12 g	Instant Yeast
4 tsp	12 g	Salt (DC kosher)
1 TBS	10 g	Shallots, minced, (optional) (or 1 tsp Onion Powder)
½ C	60 g	Whole Wheat Flour
2 C	240 g	Rye Flour
4¼ C	510 g	Bread Flour (approx)
1 TBS	11 g	Cornmeal or Semolina for dusting pans

- Pour hot water over espresso and seeds in a large mixing bowl.
- Add chocolate (broken into pieces) and stir to melt.
- Stir in room temperature water, oil, molasses and vinegar.
- Mix in 2½ C of bread flour; beat well.
- With batter temperature under 110°F, mix in yeast.
- Optionally, let batter rest 15~30 minutes (autolyse) while sponge develops.
- Mix in salt and shallots (if desired).
- Beat in whole wheat and rye, one cup at a time.
- Mix in more bread flour, ¼ C at a time, until dough starts to release from bowl.
- Dust dough and counter lightly with bread flour and turn dough out.
- Knead until dough is smooth and elastic, adding flour only as necessary.
- Rise, covered, in a lightly oiled bowl until doubled in bulk.
- Preheat oven to 375°F while dough rises.
- Fold dough on itself a few times; knead briefly; divide in half.
- Prepare pan with parchment (optional).
- Sprinkle pan with cornmeal or semolina.
- Shape dough into loaves and place on prepared pan.
- Rise, covered, until almost doubled. Do not allow to over-rise!
- Dust loaves with rye and slash just before baking.
- Bake 35 ~ 40 minutes until done.
- Cool on a wire rack before cutting or storing.

BUCHTY
Slovakian Breakfast Treats

1½ C	366 g	Milk, scalded
½ C	113 g	Butter/Margarine (1 stick)
½ C	100 g	Sugar
3 large	57 g	Egg yolks, beaten
4 tsp	12 g	Instant Yeast
4 tsp	12 g	Salt (DC kosher)
1 tsp	4 g	Vanilla Extract (optional)
2 tsp	4 g	Lemon Zest (optional)
6 C	720 g	All-Purpose Flour (approx)
¼ C	57 g	Butter (½ stick) for coating
4 T	31 g	Confectioners' Sugar

- Warm eggs in hot tap water while you continue.
- Scald milk in saucepan or microwave to 180°F.
- Add butter/margarine to hot milk to melt; then dissolve sugar in milk mixture.
- In a large bowl, beat egg yolks.
- Add milk mixture to beaten eggs (temper).
- Mix in 2 C of flour; beat well by hand or with mixer.
- With batter temperature under 110°F, mix in yeast.
- Optionally, let batter rest 15~30 minutes (autolyse) while sponge develops.
- Mix in salt, flavorings, and then 2 additional C of flour, one cup at a time.
- Mix in more flour, ¼ C at a time, until dough starts to release from bowl.
- Dust dough and counter lightly with flour and turn dough out.
- Knead until dough is smooth and elastic, adding flour only as necessary.
- Rise, covered, in a lightly oiled bowl until doubled in bulk.
- Lightly grease the sides of two 8-inch square cake pans.
- Line the bottoms of the pans with parchment cut to fit.
- Fold dough on itself a few times; knead briefly; divide in half.
- Divide each half into 16 round pieces.
- Coat each "buchta" with butter and place into prepared pans.
- Allow dough to rise, covered, until almost but not quite doubled.
- Preheat oven to 375°F while dough rises.
- Brush tops with butter (optional).
- Bake 25~30 minutes until golden and just done; do not over-bake.
- Remove from pans; cool on a wire rack.
- Dust with confectioners' sugar before separating into rolls.

> **Recipe Tip**
> Try these with a teaspoon of jam or pastry filling inside each roll.

KOLACHE
Czech Filled Pastries

1¼ C	295 g	Warm Water (120°~130°F)
½ C	100 g	Sugar or Honey
⅓ C	23 g	Instant Dry Milk
2¼ C	270 g	Unbleached Pastry Flour
1 TBS	9 g	Instant Yeast
1 TBS	10 g	Salt (DC kosher)
1 tsp	4 g	Vanilla Extract (optional)
½ tsp	1 g	Mace or Nutmeg (optional)
6 TBS	85 g	Butter, softened
2 large	38 g	Egg Yolks, separated and beaten
3¼ C	390 g	Unbleached A-P Flour (approx)
Egg wash		Egg white beaten with 1 TBS Water

> **Recipe Tip**
> Try layered fillings with some cream cheese on the bottom and fruit preserves on top.

- Warm eggs in hot tap water while you continue.
- Measure warm water into a large mixing bowl.
- Mix sugar and milk into the water.
- Beat in 2¼ C of pastry flour to make a batter.
- Check batter temperature; when under 110°F mix in yeast.
- Let batter rest 15~30 minutes (autolyse) while sponge develops.
- Mix in salt, spices, butter, and egg yolks.
- Mix in 2½ C of A-P flour, half at a time.
- Mix in more flour, 2 TBS at a time, until dough starts to release from bowl.
- Dust dough and counter lightly with flour and turn dough out.
- Knead until dough is smooth and elastic, adding flour only as necessary.
- Rise, covered, in a lightly oiled bowl until doubled in bulk.
- Line 2 sheet pans with parchment.
- Fold dough on itself a few times; knead briefly; divide in half.
- Divide each half into 10 equal size pieces.
- Shape pieces into smooth balls.
- Roll dough balls out to ~½ inch high.
- Let dough rise ~ 20 minutes to almost double.
- Preheat oven to 350°F while dough rises.
- Using 2 fingers on each hand, stretch an indentation in each pastry.
- Add 1~2 tsp of filling to the indentations; do not overfill.
- Place filled pastries onto a prepared pan; repeat with other half of dough.
- Allow dough to rise, loosely covered, another 10 minutes.
- Brush tops with egg wash (optional) if a glossy finish is desired.
- Bake ~20 minutes until golden and just done; do not over-bake.
- Remove from pans; cool on a wire rack.
- Optionally, dust with confectioners' sugar when cool.

RICOTTA OLIVE BOLSO

Dough

1½ C	354 g	Warm Water (120°~130°F)
⅓ C	23 g	Instant Dry Milk (optional)
1 TBS	13 g	Sugar (or Honey)
2¼ tsp	7 g	Instant Yeast (1 packet)
2 tsp	7 g	Salt (DC kosher)
2 TBS	28 g	Oil (or butter)
4 C	480 g	Unbleached Flour (approx)
2 TBS	21 g	Semolina for pan
Egg wash		Egg beaten with 1 TBS Water

Filling

1 large	50 g	Egg, beaten
1 C	113 g	Cheddar Cheese, grated
¾ C	100 g	Green Olives, sliced
15 oz	425 g	Ricotta Cheese
½ tsp	1 g	Oregano (dried)
pinch	1 g	Black Pepper (to taste)
1~2 cloves	2 g	Garlic, minced

Recipe Tip
Try substituting Kalamata olives or a 50/50 mix with green olives for great flavor.

- Measure warm water into a large mixing bowl.
- Mix in milk and sugar; beat in 2 C flour to make a batter.
- Check batter temperature; when under 110°F mix in yeast.
- Let batter rest 10~20 minutes (autolyse) while sponge develops.
- Mix in salt and oil; then mix in 1½ C flour, half at a time.
- Mix in more flour, 2 TBS at a time, until dough starts to release from bowl.
- Dust dough and counter lightly with flour and turn dough out.
- Knead until dough is smooth and elastic, adding flour only as necessary.
- Rise, covered, in a lightly oiled bowl until doubled in bulk.
- While dough rises, mix filling ingredients.
- Prepare 2 sheet pans with parchment (optional); sprinkle with semolina.
- Fold dough on itself a few times; knead briefly; divide into 12 equal pieces.
- Roll into smooth balls; then roll or pat balls out into ovals or rectangles.
- Place ~ 3 TBS of filling on one half; fold dough over to cover; seal edges.
- Place filled bolso on prepared pan; repeat process with other pieces.
- Preheat oven to 375°F while dough rises.
- Rise, covered, about 20 minutes.
- For a glossy finish, brush with egg wash just before baking.
- Bake ~ 35 minutes until golden and done.
- Enjoy warm or cool completely on a wire rack before storing.

Ingredients by Edward Espé Brown

ZÜPFE
Swiss Braided Bread

2 large	100 g	Eggs, warmed then beaten
2 C	488 g	Warm Milk (120°~130°F)
1 TBS	21 g	Honey or sugar
6⅓ C	760 g	All-Purpose Flour (approx)
1 TBS	10 g	Instant Yeast
1 TBS	10 g	Salt (DC kosher)
½ C	114 g	Butter, softened (1 stick)
Egg wash		1 Egg Yolk beaten with 1 TBS Water

- Warm eggs in hot tap water while you continue.
- Measure warm milk into a large bowl.
- Mix in honey/sugar.
- Mix in 3 C of flour; stir briskly until smooth.
- With batter temperature under 110°F, mix in yeast.
- Optionally, let batter rest 15~30 minutes (autolyse) while sponge develops.
- Mix in salt, beaten eggs, and butter; mix in 3 C of flour, one at a time.
- Mix in additional flour, 2 TBS at a time, until dough starts to release from bowl.
- Dust dough and counter lightly with flour and turn dough out.
- Knead until dough is smooth and elastic, adding flour only as necessary.
- Shape dough into a tight ball.
- Rise, covered, in a lightly oiled bowl until doubled in bulk.
- Fold dough on itself a few times and knead briefly.
- Preheat oven to 375°F while you continue with the recipe.
- Prepare sheet pan with parchment; spray with release (PAM).
- Using bench scraper, divide dough into 4 equal pieces.
- Roll each piece into a 18-inch long rope.
- Using 2 ropes, create a cross.
- Fold the top end of the bottom rope between the two lower ends.
- Fold remaining top end down so all 4 ropes are pointed downward.
- Start on the left and braid the first over second and third over fourth.
- Continue braiding to form a loaf; tuck ends underneath.
- Place complete loaf on prepared pan.
- Repeat braiding process with other 2 ropes to create a second loaf.
- Rise, covered, until almost but not quite doubled.
- Brush with egg wash just before baking.
- Bake 30~35 minutes until golden and just done; do not over-bake.
- Cool on a wire rack before cutting or storing.

PARATHA
Unleavened Indian-style Whole Wheat Flatbread

1 C	120 g	All-Purpose Flour
1 C	120 g	Whole Wheat Flour
1 tsp	3 g	Salt (DC kosher)
1 C	236 g	Warm Water (120°F)
1 TBS	14 g	Oil

- Blend A-P flour, W/W flour, and salt in a mixing bowl.
- Mix in water until you have a kneadable dough.
- Dough should be soft but not wet.
- Lightly oil your hand and knead dough in the bowl for 3 minutes.
- Allow dough to rest, covered, 5~10 minutes.
- While dough rests, preheat griddle or skillet to medium-high.
- Knead briefly and divide dough into 8~10 chestnut-size pieces.
- Form pieces into round dough balls by rolling between your palms.
- Coat a dough ball with slight dusting of flour.
- Roll the dough ball into a 3-inch round.
- Brush with a drop or two of oil and fold in half.
- Brush the half with a drop of oil and fold in half again.
- Repeat this process with the other pieces of dough.
- Coat a dough piece on both sides with slight dusting of flour.
- Then roll it out to a 5-inch circle (crepe-thick).
- Repeat the rolling process with a few more pieces.
- Bake on griddle or skillet to golden spots, about a minute/side.
- Store in covered bowl to keep soft and warm until served.
- Complete rolling and baking of remaining pieces.

Recipe Tip
- For fresh bread on a hot summer day, try baking Indian flatbread on the grill. You won't heat up the kitchen, and the bread will have nice grill marks!

NAAN
Leavened Indian-style Whole Wheat Flatbread

1 C	236 g	Warm Water (120°F)
1½ C	180 g	All-Purpose or Bread Flour
1 tsp	4 g	Sugar
1 tsp	3 g	Instant Yeast
1 tsp	3 g	Salt (DC kosher)
2 TBS	27 g	Oil (or melted butter/margarine)
2 TBS	31 g	Yogurt (optional)
1 C	120 g	Whole Wheat Flour

- Measure warm water into a mixing bowl.
- Mix in 1 C of A-P flour (not all of it!) and sugar and beat well.
- With batter temperature under 110°F, mix in yeast.
- Optionally, let batter rest 15~30 minutes (autolyse) while sponge develops.
- Mix in salt, oil, yogurt, and whole wheat flour.
- Mix in slightly more A-P flour until dough is just kneadable.
- Knead right in the bowl for a few minutes.
- Rise, covered, in oiled bowl 30~60 minutes.
- If using a stone, preheat oven + stone to 475°F while dough rises.
- Fold dough on itself a few times and knead briefly.
- Divide dough into 6 equal size pieces.
- Form pieces into round dough balls by rolling between your palms.
- Allow dough to rest 5~10 minutes.
- If not using a stone, preheat griddle or skillet to medium-high.
- Using a pin, roll dough balls out into 8-inch circles.
- Bake to golden, about 2~3 min/side.
- Enjoy warm or cool before storing.

INTERNATIONAL

PITA BREAD
Turkish Flatbread Pockets

1 C	236 g	Warm Water (120°~130°F)
2 tsp	6 g	Instant Yeast
2 tsp	7 g	Salt (DC kosher)
1 TBS	14 g	Extra Virgin Olive Oil
2¾ C	330 g	All-Purpose Flour (approx)
2 TBS	15 g	Flour for dusting counter

> **Recipe Tip**
> For healthier pitas, substitute up to half the flour with whole wheat.

- Measure warm water into a medium size mixing bowl.
- Mix in 1½ C of flour; stir briskly until smooth.
- With batter temperature under 110°F, mix in yeast.
- Optionally, let batter rest 15~30 minutes (autolyse) while sponge develops.
- Mix in salt, oil, and then 1 C of flour.
- Mix in additional flour, 1 TBS at a time, until dough starts to release from bowl.
- Dust dough and counter lightly with flour and turn dough out.
- Knead until dough is smooth and elastic, adding flour only as necessary.
- Rise, covered, in a lightly oiled bowl until doubled in bulk.
- Preheat oven and stone or 2 sheet pans to 450°F while dough rises.
- Fold dough on itself a few times; knead briefly; divide into 6 equal pieces.
- If oven space is limited, shape and bake only 2 or 3 at a time.
- Initially, shape dough into round balls.
- Let dough rest, covered, 5~10 minutes.
- Prepare bread board or counter with a sprinkle with flour.
- Flatten balls and roll into rounds ¼-inch thick, 6~7 inches in diameter.
- Place rounds on floured surface; allow to rise, covered, 20~30 minutes.
- Transfer rounds to pre-heated stone or sheet pans.
- Bake in hot oven ~5 minutes until done.
- Pitas should puff up in the oven; they do not need to brown.
- Cover with a lint-free towel to keep pitas soft and warm.
- Enjoy warm or cool completely before storing.

FLOUR TORTILLAS
"New World" Mexican Flatbreads

2 C	240 g	Unbleached All-Purpose Flour
1 tsp	3 g	Salt (DC kosher)
1 tsp	5 g	Baking Powder
¼ C	51 g	Lard, Shortening or Oil
¾ C	177 g	Water (approx)
as required		Flour for bench

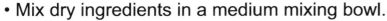

- Mix dry ingredients in a medium mixing bowl.
- Cut in lard or shortening (or mix in oil).
- Mix in water until a sticky ball forms.
- Knead dough briefly on a floured board until smooth and elastic.
- Wrap in plastic and let rest for 20~30 minutes.
- Divide dough into 6~8 equal size pieces; shape into balls, covered.
- Heat a dry griddle or heavy skillet on a medium-high burner.
- On a floured board, roll one ball out to ~ 8-inch diameter round.
- Keep other pieces of dough covered until later.
- Cook the tortilla until golden or a few brown spots form on both sides.
- Do not over-cook or they will dry out and become hard.
- Place cooked tortillas under a damp towel to keep soft.
- Repeat to shape and cook remaining tortillas.

CORN TORTILLAS
Original Mexican Flatbreads

1½ C	xx g	Masa Harina
½ tsp	2 g	Salt (DC kosher)
1 C	236 g	Water, hot from tap (approx)
as required		Flour for bench

- Mix masa harina and salt in a medium mixing bowl.
- Mix in water until a ball of dough forms.
- Knead dough briefly on a floured board until smooth and elastic.
- Wrap in plastic and let rest for 15~30 minutes.
- Divide dough into ping-pong size pieces; shape into balls.
- Heat a dry griddle or heavy skillet on a medium-high burner.
- Press or roll one ball out to ~ 6-inch diameter round.
- Cook the tortilla 1~2 minutes on each side until dry and pebbly.
- Wrap cooked tortillas in a clean towel.
- Repeat to shape and cook remaining tortillas.

BALEP KORKUN
Tibetan-style Skillet Bread

1¼ C	150 g	All-Purpose Flour
2 tsp	9 g	Baking Powder
1½ tsp	5 g	DC Kosher Salt
¾ C	177 g	Water

- Grease a 10-inch skillet.
- Preheat skillet to medium on stove top burner.
- Combine dry ingredients in a bowl.
- Mix water into dry ingredients.
- Transfer batter to skillet.
- Sprinkle 1 TBS of water around the edge of the pan to create steam.
- Cover and cook 7~8 minutes to golden.
- Flip, cover, and cook 4~5 minutes on the other side until done.
- Remove from pan; cool briefly on a wire rack before cutting.

> **Recipe Tip**
> Choose a non-stick pan for this recipe.

based on techniques by Jacques Pepin

MANAKISH
Lebanese Flat Bread

2 C	472 g	Warm Water (120°~130°F)
1 TBS	13 g	Granulated Sugar
5½ C	660 g	Bread Flour (approx)
1 TBS	10 g	Instant Yeast
1 TBS	10 g	Salt (DC kosher)
4 TBS	55 g	Olive Oil (+ more for tops)
1 TBS	11 g	Semolina for dusting pans
7 TBS	70 g	Zaatar Spice Blend

- Measure warm water into a large mixing bowl.
- Mix in sugar and 3 C of flour; stir briskly until smooth.
- With batter temperature under 110°F, mix in yeast.
- Optionally, let batter rest 15~30 minutes (autolyse) while sponge develops.
- Mix in salt, 4 TBS oil, and then 2 C of flour, one at a time.
- Mix in additional flour, ¼ C at a time, until dough starts to release from bowl.
- Dust dough and counter lightly with flour and turn dough out.
- Knead until dough is smooth and elastic, adding flour only as necessary.
- Rise, covered, in a lightly oiled bowl until doubled in bulk.
- Preheat oven and stone or sheet pan to 400°F while dough rises.
- Prepare parchment with a sprinkle with semolina.
- Fold risen dough on itself a few times; knead briefly; divide dough in half.
- Bench rest 5~10 minutes.
- Roll dough into rectangles; place dough on parchment.
- Cut diagonal slits in dough; open slits to form ovals.
- Brush tops with additional oil and sprinkle with zaatar spice blend.
- Rise, covered, until almost but not quite doubled, about 20 minutes.
- Bake 15~20 minutes until golden and done.
- Enjoy warm or cool on a wire rack before storing.

ZAATAR SPICE BLEND

4 TBS	Thyme
1 TBS	Toasted Sesame Seeds
1 TBS	Ground Sumac
1 TBS	Salt

- Combine all ingredients and mix well.
- Transfer to a shaker-top container for storage and easy use.

CHALLAH
Traditional pareve Jewish Braid

1¾ C	413 g	Warm Water (120°~130°F)
2 TBS	25 g	Sugar
7¼ C	870 g	All-Purpose Flour
4 tsp	13 g	Instant Yeast
4 tsp	13 g	Salt (DC kosher)
3 large	150 g	Eggs, beaten
¼ C	55 g	Vegetable Oil
2 TBS	21 g	Semolina for pan
Egg wash		1 Egg beaten with 1 TBS Water
1 TBS	10 g	Poppy or Sesame Seeds (optional)

- Warm eggs in hot tap water while you continue.
- Measure warm water into a large mixing bowl.
- Mix in sugar and 2½ C of flour; stir briskly until smooth.
- With batter temperature under 110°F, mix in yeast.
- Optionally, let batter rest 15~30 minutes (autolyse) while sponge develops.
- Mix in salt, 3 beaten eggs, and oil.
- Mix in 4 C of flour, one at a time; beat well.
- Mix in more flour, ¼ C at a time, until dough starts to release from bowl.
- Dust dough and counter lightly with flour and turn dough out.
- Knead until dough is smooth and elastic, adding flour only as necessary.
- Rise, covered, in a lightly oiled bowl until doubled in bulk.
- Fold dough on itself a few times; knead briefly; divide in half for 2 loaves.
- Prepare sheet pan with parchment (optional); sprinkle pan with semolina.
- Divide each half of dough into 6 equal size pieces.
- Roll pieces into ropes ~ 9 inches long.
- Roll ropes out again, this time to ~ 18 inches long.
- Braid from one side going over 2 then under 1 then over 2.
- Place loaf on prepared pan.
- Preheat oven to 375°F while dough rises.
- Rise until almost but not quite double (20~30 minutes).
- Brush with egg wash and sprinkle with seeds if desired.
- Bake 30~35 minutes until golden and done.
- Cool on a wire rack before cutting or storing.

> **Recipe Tips**
> For help braiding challah, search YouTube for a video clip.
> This bread is excellent for making French toast.

CHALLAH BRAIDING
using 6 strands

Divide dough into 6 equal size pieces.
Place on lightly floured surface.
Roll each piece out to 9 inches long.
Roll each strand out to 18 inches long.

Arrange the dough strands in a fan shape.
Pinch the strands together at the far end.

Start with strand #1 on the far right.
Pass strand #1 over two, under one, over two.
(over #2 & #3, under #4, over #5 & #6)

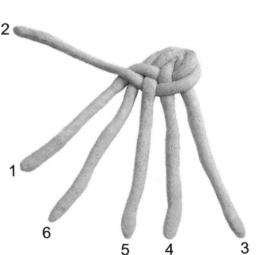

Repeat with strand #2 on the far right.
Pass strand #2 over two, under one, over two.
(over #3 & #4, under #5, over #6 & #1)

Continue braiding until loaf is complete.
Tuck any loose ends under.
Pinch ends to prevent unraveling.
Transfer to parchment-lined pan.
Brush with egg wash if desired.

ITALIAN EASTER BRAID

Dough
½ recipe   Challah Dough
Egg wash   1 Egg Yolk beaten with 1 tsp Water

Technique
- Prepare sheet pan with parchment (optional); sprinkle pan with semolina.
- Divide dough into 6 equal size pieces.
- Roll pieces into ropes ~ 9 inches long.
- Roll ropes out again, this time to ~ 18 inches long.
- Braid from one side going over 2 then under 1 then over 2.
- Pull braid into a wreath.
- Attach ends by pinching together.
- Place wreath on prepared pan.
- Preheat oven to 375°F while dough rises.
- Rise until almost but not quite double (20~30 minutes).
- Brush with egg wash.
- Bake 30~35 minutes until golden and done.
- Cool on a wire rack before cutting or storing.

> **Recipe Tip**
> Place a candle in the middle and use as the centerpiece for your table.

PANETTONE
Italian Holiday Bread

1 C	244 g	Milk, scalded
1 C	160 g	Raisins (golden preferred)
½ C	113 g	Butter/Margarine (1 stick)
½ C	100 g	Sugar
1 TBS	6 g	Lemon Zest or 2 tsp dried peel
1 TBS	6 g	Orange Zest or 2 tsp dried peel
1 TBS	13 g	Vanilla Extract
3 large	150 g	Eggs
3 large	57 g	Egg Yolks
4 tsp	12 g	Instant Yeast
4 tsp	12 g	Salt (DC kosher)
5½ C	660 g	All-Purpose Flour (approx)

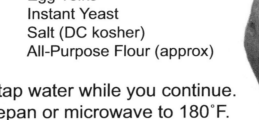

- Warm eggs in hot tap water while you continue.
- Scald milk in saucepan or microwave to 180°F.
- Add raisins to hot milk to plump.
- Add butter/margarine to hot milk, stir to melt.
- Dissolve sugar in milk mixture; then add lemon, orange, and vanilla.
- In a large bowl, beat eggs and yolks.
- Add milk mixture to eggs.
- Mix in 3 C of flour; beat well by hand or with mixer.
- With batter temperature under 110°F, mix in yeast.
- Optionally, let batter rest 15~30 minutes (autolyse) while sponge develops.
- Mix in salt and then 2 additional C of flour, one at a time.
- Mix in more flour, ¼ C at a time, until dough starts to release from bowl.
- Dust dough and counter lightly with flour and turn dough out.
- Knead until dough is smooth and elastic, adding flour only as necessary.
- Rise, covered, in a lightly oiled bowl until doubled in bulk.
- Fold dough on itself a few times; knead briefly; divide in half.
- Preheat oven to 375°F while you continue with the recipe.
- Line bottoms of two 8-inch round pans with parchment.
- Create parchment sleeves and line the sides as well.
- Shape risen dough into round loaves; place in prepared pans.
- Allow dough to rise until almost but not quite doubled.
- Optionally, brush tops with melted butter.
- Bake 40~45 minutes until golden and done.
- Tent tops with foil after 20 minutes if they are browning too rapidly.
- Remove from pans; cool on a wire rack before cutting or storing.
- When cool, optionally dust with confectioners' sugar before slicing.

BASIC ITALIAN DOUGH
1200g recipe for bread and pizza crust

1⁷/₈ C	442 g	Warm Water (120°~130°F)
1 TBS	13 g	Granulated Sugar
6 C	720 g	All-Purpose Flour (approx)
1 TBS	10 g	Instant Yeast
1 TBS	10 g	Salt (DC kosher)
¼ C	55 g	Olive Oil
1 TBS	11 g	Semolina for dusting pans

> **Recipe Tip**
> For an extra-crispy pizza crust, pre-bake 5~8 minutes until it just starts to brown.

Basic Dough
- Measure warm water into a large mixing bowl.
- Mix in sugar and 3 C of flour; stir briskly until smooth.
- With batter temperature under 110°F, mix in yeast.
- Optionally, let batter rest 15~30 minutes (autolyse) while sponge develops.
- Mix in salt, oil, and then 2¾ C of flour, one cup at a time.
- Mix in additional flour until dough just starts to release from bowl.
- Dust dough and counter lightly with flour and turn dough out.
- Knead until dough is smooth and elastic, adding flour only as necessary.
- Rise, covered, in a lightly oiled bowl until doubled in bulk.

for Loaves
- Preheat oven to 400°F while dough rises.
- Prepare pans with parchment (optional); sprinkle pans with semolina.
- Gently release risen dough from bowl and divide in half or thirds.
- Fold dough several times to tighten and shape into loaves.
- Transfer to prepared pans and allow loaves to rise briefly until puffy.
- Just before baking, slash loaves as desired with a serrated knife.
- Bake 30~35 minutes until done and a tap on the bottom sounds hollow.
- Remove from pans; cool on a wire rack before cutting or storing.

for Pizza
- Preheat oven (and baking stone if available) to 475°F while dough rises.
- Prepare pans with parchment (optional); sprinkle pans with semolina.
- Fold dough on itself a few times; knead briefly; bench rest 10~15 minutes.
- Divide dough as required.
    - 400g = 3 large pizza   300g = 4 medium pizza   200g = 6 personal pizza
- Flatten and stretch or roll dough on floured bench into rounds or rectangles.
- Place on prepared pans and stretch or roll dough to adjust fit as desired.
- Optionally, pre-bake ~ 5 minutes for an crispy crust.
- Add thin layer of sauce, grated cheese, and other toppings as desired.
- Bake in hot oven 10~15 minutes until done and cheese is melted.

STROMBOLI

22 oz	615 g	Basic Italian Dough (half of recipe on previous page)
7~8 oz	200 g	Sliced Meats: Ham, Salami, Pepperoni
4~5 oz	125 g	Sliced or Shredded Italian Cheeses
1 TBS	11 g	Semolina for dusting pan

- Preheat oven (and stone if you have one) to 375°F while you continue.
- Prepare sheet pan with parchment (optional) and dust with semolina.
- Flatten dough; roll or stretch out to a 10-inch tall x 16-inch wide rectangle.
- Top middle of dough with layers of meats and cheeses.
- Fold in thirds with 2-inch overlap; pinch seams to seal; fold ends over on top.
- Turn over and place seam-side-down on prepared sheet pan.
- Brush stromboli with olive oil; cut several vents in the top.
- Bake 25~30 minutes until done; slide off pan onto rack for last 10 minutes.
- Cool briefly; slice into servings for appetizers or entrees.

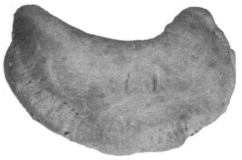

CALZONES
makes 2

22 oz	615 g	Basic Italian Dough (half of recipe on previous page)
6 oz	170 g	Sliced Meats: Ham, Salami, Pepperoni
4 oz	113 g	Sliced or Shredded Italian Cheeses
1 TBS	11 g	Semolina for dusting pan

- Preheat oven (and stone if you have one) to 375°F while you continue.
- Prepare sheet pan with parchment (optional) and dust with semolina.
- Divide dough into 2 equal size pieces (10~12 oz each).
- Flatten dough; roll or stretch out to a 7-inch wide x 12-inch tall oval.
- Cover bottom half with layers of meats and cheeses; leave half-inch border.
- Fold top half dough down to cover fillings; pinch seams to seal well.
- Place on prepared pan; repeat with other piece of dough.
- Brush calzones with olive oil; cut 1 or 2 small vents in the top of each.
- Bake 20~25 minutes until golden and done.
- Serve hot with warmed marinara sauce on top as desired.

RUSTIC ITALIAN BOULE
no-knead recipe

1½ C	354 g	Warm Water (120°~130°F)
3¾ C	450 g	Bread Flour (approx)
2 tsp	7 g	Instant Yeast
2 tsp	7 g	Salt (DC kosher)
1 TBS	11 g	Semolina for dusting pan
2 tsp	9 g	Olive Oil - optional
½ tsp	2 g	Coarse Sea Salt - optional

- In a large bowl, mix 2 C of flour into water.
- With batter under 110°F mix in yeast; stir briskly until smooth.
- Optionally, let batter rest 15~30 minutes (autolyse) while sponge develops.
- Beat in salt and then remaining flour, a half-cup at a time.
- Dough will be too sticky to handle. Do not over flour.
- Rise, covered, until doubled, 30~40 minutes.
- Optionally, rise dough on a floured towel in a wicker basket.
- Preheat oven (and baking stone if available) to 500°F.
- Lightly oil a heavy 9-inch skillet (or two smaller ones) and dust with semolina.
- Gently transfer dough to skillet without deflating.
- Allow bread to rise briefly 10~20 minutes after transferring to pan.
- Spray or brush loaf with water (for hard crust) or olive oil (for soft crust).
- Optionally, sprinkle top with coarse salt if desired.
- Score bread in a pattern of your choosing (see diagrams in appendix).
- Put bread into oven and reduce temp to 450°F.
- Bake 30~35 minutes until done and a tap on the bottom sounds hollow.
- Cool on a wire rack before cutting or storing.

> Recipe Tip
> Use a stand mixer with the flat beater for this recipe.

RUSTIC ITALIAN BOULE
rising, scoring, and baking the loaf

Line a wicker basket with a lint-free towel.
Dust the towel with flour.
Place your dough in the basket to rise.
Place the basket inside a large plastic bag.
Remove it when it has almost doubled in bulk.

Spray the skillet lightly with release (PAM).
Sprinkle the skillet with semolina to coat.
Place the skillet over the risen dough.

Invert the basket and skillet in one motion.
This will transfer the dough to the skillet.

Remove the basket to reveal the dough.
The dough should have a coating of flour.
If necessary, dust dough lightly with flour.

Score the dough in a pattern of your choice.
Use a lame or very sharp knife.
Cut dough only about a quarter-inch deep.

Place skillet in oven on a pre-heated stone.

After 20 minutes, remove bread from skillet.
Finish baking the bread on the stone.

FOCACCIA

2 C	472 g	Warm Water (120°~130°F)
5¼ C	630 g	Bread Flour (approx)
1 TBS	10 g	Instant Yeast
1 TBS	10 g	Salt (DC kosher)
2 TBS	28 g	Extra Virgin Olive Oil for dough
1 TBS	11 g	Semolina for dusting parchment or pans
1 TBS	14 g	Extra Virgin Olive Oil for topping (approx)
2 TBS	4 g	Fresh Rosemary, chopped (optional, for topping)
1 tsp	3 g	Coarse Sea Salt (optional, for topping)

- Measure warm water into a large mixing bowl.
- Mix in 3 C of flour; stir briskly until smooth.
- With batter temperature under 110°F, mix in yeast.
- Optionally, let batter rest 15~30 minutes (autolyse) while sponge develops.
- Mix in salt, 2 TBS oil, and then 2 C of flour, one at a time.
- Dust dough and counter lightly with ¼ C flour and turn dough out.
- Stretch and fold to knead; dough should be sticky inside; do not over flour.
- Rise, covered, until doubled in bulk, 30~40 minutes.
- Preheat oven (and baking stone if available) to 450°F while dough rises.
- Prepare parchment or two sheet pans with a generous sprinkle of semolina.
- Divide dough in half (for two loaves).
- Stretch / roll / press dough out to ¾-inch thick.
- Transfer dough to prepared parchment or pans.
- Brush (or spray) top of dough with olive oil.
- Insert finger tips straight down into dough; make random indentations all over.
- Sprinkle with toppings: rosemary and/or coarse sea salt.
- Additional rise is not necessary; bake to golden brown color, 15~20 minutes.
- Enjoy warm or cool on a wire rack before storing.

Recipe Tips

- For a nice savory focaccia, top with grated asiago cheese and sprinkle with chopped chives.

- For breakfast focaccia, substitute butter for oil (in dough and on top) and dust with cinnamon sugar. Use light brown sugar for even more flavor.

ROSEMARY & OLIVE OIL BREAD

2~3 TBS	4 g	Fresh Rosemary, chopped fine
¼ C	55 g	Extra Virgin Olive Oil
1¾ C	413 g	Warm Water (120°~130°F)
¼ C	60 g	Rye Flour (or whole wheat if you prefer)
1 TBS	10 g	Instant Yeast
1 TBS	10 g	Salt (DC kosher)
4¼ C	510 g	Bread Flour (approx)
1 TBS	11 g	Semolina for dusting pans
1 tsp	3 g	Coarse Sea Salt (optional, for topping)

- Strip leaves from 2 long branches of fresh rosemary.
- Chop the leaves finely.
- Gently warm the olive oil in a small saucepan to 160°~180°F.
- Take off-heat and stir in the rosemary; it should not sizzle (fry)!
- Steep rosemary in warm oil while you continue with the recipe.
- Measure warm water into a large mixing bowl.
- Mix in rye and 2 C of bread flour; stir briskly until smooth.
- With batter temperature under 110°F, mix in yeast.
- Let batter rest 15~30 minutes (autolyse) while sponge develops.
- Mix salt, oil and rosemary into the sponge.
- Mix in 2 C of bread flour, one at a time; beat well.
- Dust dough and counter lightly with remaining ¼ C flour and turn out.
- Stretch and fold to knead; dough should be sticky inside; do not over flour.
- Rise, covered, until doubled in bulk, 30~40 minutes.
- Preheat oven (and baking stone if available) to 475°F while dough rises.
- Dust parchment, sheet pan, or 2 oven-proof skillets with semolina.
- Gently release risen dough from bowl and divide in half.
- Fold dough several times to tighten and shape into oblong or round loaves.
- Transfer to prepared pan and allow loaves to rise briefly until puffy.
- Optionally, brush loaves with olive oil and sprinkle with coarse salt.
- Just before baking, slash loaves as desired with a serrated knife.
- Put into hot oven and reduce temp to 425°F.
- Bake to golden brown color and done, about 25~30 minutes.
- Cool on a wire rack before cutting or storing.

> Recipe Tips
> - Don't be tempted to make bread with dried rosemary. Use fresh!
> - You can also preferment half the dough for even more flavor.

RUSTIC ITALIAN

PANE RUSTICO

Poolish Preferment

1 C	236 g	Room Temperature Water (75°F)
2 C	240 g	Bread Flour (can include 2~3 TBS Rye or Whole Wheat)
¼ tsp	¾ g	Instant Yeast

- Combine water, flour, and yeast in a non-reactive container; stir well.
- Cover loosely, permitting gas to escape.
- Allow to ferment 6~8 hours at room temperature.

Bread

Preferment	(all)	From Day Before
1 C	236 g	Very Hot Water (200°F)
2¾ C	330 g	Bread Flour (approx)
1 TBS	10 g	Instant Yeast
1 TBS	10 g	Salt (DC kosher)
1 TBS	11 g	Semolina for dusting pan

- Transfer preferment into a large mixing bowl.
- Mix in hot water and then 1½ C of flour.
- With batter temperature under 110°F, mix in yeast.
- Optionally, let batter rest 15~30 minutes (autolyse) while sponge develops.
- Mix in salt; then mix in 1 C of additional flour, a half-cup at a time; beat well.
- Dust dough and counter lightly with remaining ¼ C flour and turn out.
- Stretch and fold to knead; dough should be sticky inside; do not over flour.
- Rise, covered, until doubled in bulk, 30~40 minutes.
- Preheat oven (and baking stone if available) to 450°F while dough rises.
- Dust parchment, sheet pan, or 2 oven-proof skillets with semolina.
- Gently release risen dough from bowl and divide in half.
- Fold dough several times to tighten and shape into oblong or round loaves.
- Degas dough as little as possible during folding and shaping.
- Transfer to prepared pan and allow loaves to rise briefly until puffy.
- Just before baking, slash loaves as desired with a serrated knife.
- Mist loaves with water just before baking and twice more at 3-minute intervals.
- Bake to golden brown color and done, about 25~30 minutes.
- Cool on a wire rack before cutting or storing.

> **Recipe Tips**
> Incorporating a preferment can add character and depth of flavor, stronger gluten structure, and better keeping quality to your bread. Poolish style preferments are easy to incorporate by hand, and a biga style preferment can be used when a stand mixer is available.

FILONCINO INTEGRALE

Poolish Preferment

1 C	236 g	Room Temperature Water (75°F)
1¼ C	150 g	Bread Flour
½ C	60 g	Rye Flour
¼ tsp	¾ g	Instant Yeast

- Combine water, flours, and yeast in a non-reactive container; stir well.
- Cover loosely, permitting gas to escape.
- Allow to ferment 6~8 hours at room temperature.

Bread

Preferment	(all)	From Day Before
1 C	236 g	Very Hot Water (200°F)
2¼ C	270 g	Bread Flour (approx)
1 TBS	10 g	Instant Yeast
1 TBS	10 g	Salt (DC kosher)
¾ C	90 g	Whole Wheat Flour
2 TBS	21 g	Semolina or coarse rye

- Transfer preferment into a large mixing bowl.
- Mix in hot water and then 1 C of bread flour.
- With batter temperature under 110°F, mix in yeast.
- Optionally, allow batter to rest 15~30 minutes (autolyse) while sponge develops.
- Mix in salt; then mix in whole wheat flour.
- Mix in 1 C additional bread flour a half-cup at a time.
- Dust dough and counter lightly with remaining ¼ C flour and turn out.
- Stretch and fold to knead; dough should be sticky inside; do not over flour.
- Rise, covered, until doubled in bulk, 30~40 minutes.
- Preheat oven (and baking stone if available) to 475°F while dough rises.
- Dust parchment, sheet pan, or 2 oven-proof skillets with semolina.
- Gently release risen dough from bowl and divide in half.
- Fold dough several times to tighten and shape into oblong or round loaves.
- Transfer to prepared pan and allow loaves to rise briefly until puffy.
- Just before baking, slash loaves as desired with a serrated knife.
- Put bread into oven and reduce temp to 425°F.
- Bake to golden brown color and done, about 25~30 minutes.
- Cool on a wire rack before cutting or storing.

> **Recipe Tip**
> Don't like rye? You can substitute whole wheat in the preferment.

SEMOLINA BREAD

Poolish Preferment

1 C	236 g	Room Temperature Water (75°F)
1 C	120 g	All-Purpose Flour
½ C	84 g	Semolina Flour
¼ tsp	¾ g	Instant Yeast

> **Recipe Tip**
> Look for semolina in the pasta aisle at your market.

- Combine water, flours, and yeast in a non-reactive container; stir well.
- Cover loosely, permitting gas to escape.
- Allow to ferment 6~8 hours at room temperature.

Bread

Preferment	(all)	From Day Before
1 C	236 g	Very Hot Water (200°F)
1 C	168 g	Semolina Flour
1 TBS	10 g	Instant Yeast
1 TBS	10 g	Salt (DC kosher)
2 TBS	27 g	Olive Oil
2¼ C	270 g	All-Purpose Flour (approx)
2 TBS	20 g	Sesame Seeds (optional)
1 TBS	11 g	Semolina for pan

- Transfer preferment into a large mixing bowl.
- Mix in hot water and then mix in semolina flour.
- With batter temperature under 110°F, mix in yeast.
- Let batter rest 15~30 minutes (autolyse) while sponge develops.
- Mix in salt and oil.
- Mix 2 C of A-P flour one at a time.
- Mix in additional A-P flour as required until dough barely comes together.
- Dust dough and counter lightly with remaining ¼ C of A-P flour and turn out.
- Stretch and fold to knead; dough should be sticky inside; do not over flour.
- Rise, covered, until doubled in bulk, 30~40 minutes.
- Preheat oven (and baking stone if available) to 475°F while dough rises.
- Dust parchment, sheet pan, or 2 oven-proof skillets with semolina.
- Gently release risen dough from bowl and divide in half.
- Fold dough several times to tighten and shape into oblong or round loaves.
- Degas dough as little as possible during folding and shaping.
- Transfer to prepared pan and allow loaves to rise briefly until puffy.
- Just before baking, mist with water, sprinkle with seeds, and slash as desired.
- Put bread into oven and reduce temp to 425°F.
- Bake to golden brown color and done, about 25~30 minutes.
- Cool on a wire rack before cutting or storing.

CIABATTA

Biga Preferment

½ C	118 g	Room Temperature Water (75°F)
1½ C	180 g	Bread Flour
¼ tsp	¾ g	Instant Yeast

> **Recipe Tips**
> This recipe uses a stand mixer to incorporate the firm biga preferment into the batter. Mixing by hand is not recommended.

- Combine water and half of flour in mixer work bowl.
- Mix yeast thoroughly into batter.
- Mix in remaining flour to create a moist dough.
- Transfer to non-reactive container; cover loosely, permitting gas to escape.
- Ferment 6~8 hours at room temperature to at least double in bulk.

Bread

Biga	(all)	From Day Before (~ 1 C)
1½ C	354 g	Very Hot Water (200°F)
3¼ C	390 g	Bread Flour
1 TBS	10 g	Instant Yeast
1 TBS	10 g	Salt (DC kosher)
2 TBS	21 g	Semolina or flour for pan

- Transfer biga into the mixer work bowl.
- Mix in hot water and then mix in 2 C of flour to create a batter.
- With batter temperature under 110°F, mix in yeast.
- Let batter rest for 15~30 minutes (autolyse) while sponge develops.
- Mix in salt.
- Mix in 1 C of additional flour, a half-cup at a time, on low~medium speed.
- Dust dough and counter with remaining ¼ C flour and turn out.
- Stretch and fold to knead, using a bench scraper initially as required.
- Dough will be wet and almost pourable; resist temptation to add more flour.
- Divide dough in half and place into 2 separate bowls.
- Rise, covered, until doubled in bulk, 30~45 minutes.
- Preheat oven (and baking stone if available) to 500°F while dough rises.
- Dust sheet pan with semolina or flour; do not use cornmeal.
- Gently release dough from bowl with rubber spatula.
- Fold dough on itself to tighten and transfer onto prepared pan.
- Stretch dough out and fold ends toward center into the shape of a slipper.
- Allow shaped loaves to rise briefly until puffy.
- Do not slash! Mist loaves, put into oven, and reduce temp to 450°F.
- Bake to golden brown color and done, about 25~30 minutes.
- Cool on a wire rack before cutting or storing.

Hydration = Water/Flour = (118+354)/(180+390) = 472/570 = 83%

ROASTED GARLIC BREAD

Poolish Preferment

1 C	236 g	Room Temperature Water (75°F)
1½ C	180 g	Bread Flour
⅓ C	40 g	Rye Flour or Whole Wheat or 50/50 mix
¼ tsp	¾ g	Instant Yeast

- Combine water, flours, and yeast in a non-reactive container; stir well.
- Cover loosely, permitting gas to escape.
- Allow to ferment 6~8 hours at room temperature.

Bread

½ C	20 g	Garlic, peeled (20 cloves)
1 tsp	5 g	Olive Oil
Preferment	(all)	From Day Before
1 C	236 g	Very Hot Water (200°F)
3¼ C	390 g	Bread Flour (approx)
1 TBS	10 g	Instant Yeast
1 TBS	10 g	Salt (DC kosher)
1 tsp	3 g	Coarse Sea Salt (optional)
1 TBS	11 g	Semolina for dusting pans

Recipe Tip
To save time with this recipe you can buy pre-peeled whole garlic cloves at most markets.

- Toss garlic in olive oil, wrap in foil, bake 20~30 minutes at 350°F.
- Transfer preferment into a large mixing bowl.
- Mix in hot water and then 1½ C of flour.
- With batter temperature under 110°F, mix in yeast.
- Let batter rest for 15~30 minutes (autolyse) while sponge develops.
- Mix in salt and coarsely chopped roasted garlic.
- Mix in 1½ C of additional flour, half at a time.
- Dust dough and counter lightly with remaining ¼ C of flour and turn out.
- Stretch and fold to knead; dough will be sticky inside; do not over flour.
- Rise, covered, until doubled in bulk, 30~45 minutes.
- Preheat oven (and baking stone if available) to 450°F while dough rises.
- Dust parchment, sheet pan, or 2 oven-proof skillets with semolina.
- Gently release risen dough from bowl and divide in half.
- Fold dough several times to tighten and shape into oblong or round loaves.
- Allow loaves to rise briefly on prepared pan until puffy.
- Optionally, brush loaves with olive oil and sprinkle with coarse salt.
- Just before baking, slash loaves as desired with serrated knife.
- Bake to golden brown color and done, about 25~30 minutes.
- Cool on a wire rack before cutting or storing.

KALAMATA OLIVE BREAD

Poolish Preferment

1 C	236 g	Room Temperature Water (75°F)
1½ C	180 g	Bread Flour
⅓ C	40 g	Rye Flour or Whole Wheat or 50/50 mix
¼ tsp	¾ g	Instant Yeast

- Combine water, flours, and yeast in a non-reactive container; stir well.
- Cover loosely, permitting gas to escape.
- Allow to ferment 6~8 hours at room temperature.

Bread

Preferment	(all)	From Day Before
½ C	118 g	Boiling Hot Water (212°F)
3¼ C	390 g	Bread Flour (approx)
1 TBS	10 g	Instant Yeast
1 C	170 g	Kalamata Olives, pitted
½ C	118 g	Olive Brine
1 TBS	11 g	Semolina for dusting pans

- Transfer preferment into a large bowl.
- Mix in hot water and 1 C of flour.
- With batter temperature under 110°F, mix in yeast.
- Let batter rest for 15~30 minutes (autolyse) while sponge develops.
- Cut olives in half (along long axis); warm olives and brine to 100°F.
- Mix olives and brine into batter; add kosher salt (1~2 tsp) only if required.
- Beat in 2 C of additional flour, one at a time.
- Dust dough and counter lightly with remaining ¼ C of flour and turn out.
- Stretch and fold to knead; dough will be sticky inside; do not over flour.
- Rise, covered, until doubled in bulk, 30~45 minutes.
- Preheat oven (and baking stone if available) to 450°F while dough rises.
- Dust parchment, sheet pan, or 2 oven-proof skillets with semolina.
- Gently release risen dough from bowl and divide in half.
- Fold dough several times to tighten and shape into oblong or round loaves.
- Allow loaves to rise briefly on prepared pan until puffy.
- Just before baking, slash loaves as desired with serrated knife.
- Bake to golden brown color and done, about 25~30 minutes.
- Cool on a wire rack before cutting or storing.

> **Recipe Tip**
> When possible, choose a brine without vinegar.
> Add kosher salt if required by a weak brine.

SICILIAN SCROLL

Poolish Preferment

1 C	236 g	Room Temperature Water (75°F)
1 C	120 g	Bread Flour
½ C	84 g	Semolina Flour
¼ tsp	¾ g	Instant Yeast

- Combine water, flours, and yeast in a non-reactive container; stir well.
- Cover loosely, permitting gas to escape.
- Allow to ferment 6~8 hours at room temperature.

Bread

1 C	236 g	Boiling Hot Water (212°F)
1 C	168 g	Fine Semolina Flour
Preferment	(all)	From Day Before
1 TBS	10 g	Instant Yeast
1 TBS	10 g	Salt (DC kosher)
2 TBS	27 g	Olive Oil
2 C	240 g	Bread Flour (approx)
4 TBS	40 g	Sesame Seeds
1 TBS	11 g	Semolina for pan

- Measure hot water into a large mixing bowl.
- Mix in semolina flour; let sit 5 minutes to soften.
- Stir in preferment; mix well.
- With batter temperature under 110°F, mix in yeast.
- Let batter rest 10~20 minutes (autolyse) while sponge develops.
- Mix in salt and oil.
- Mix 1½ C of bread flour half at a time.
- Mix in additional bread flour as required until dough starts to come together.
- Dust dough and counter lightly with flour and turn out.
- Stretch and fold to knead; dough should be sticky inside; do not over flour.
- Rise, covered, in lightly oiled bowl until doubled in bulk.
- Preheat oven (and baking stone if available) to 475°F while dough rises.
- Dust parchment or sheet pan with semolina.
- Gently release risen dough from bowl and divide in half.
- Fold dough several times to tighten, roll, and form into "S" shaped loaves.
- Transfer loaves to prepared pan and allow to rise until not quite doubled.
- Just before baking, mist with water and sprinkle heavily with seeds.
- Put loaves into oven and reduce temp to 425°F.
- Bake to golden brown color and done, about 25~30 minutes.
- Cool on a wire rack before cutting or storing.

PANE CARASAU
Sardinian Flat Bread

1½ C	354 g	Warm Water (120°F)
4½ C	480 g	Bread Flour (approx) OR up to half durum flour
1 TBS	10 g	Instant Yeast
1 tsp	3 g	Salt (DC kosher)

- Measure warm water into a large mixing bowl.
- Mix in 2 C of flour; stir or whisk briskly until smooth.
- With batter temperature under 110°F, mix in yeast and stir well.
- Optionally, let batter rest 10~15 minutes (autolyse) while sponge develops.
- Mix in salt and then 1½ C of flour; mix well.
- Mix in additional flour, ¼ C at a time, until dough releases from bowl.
- Dust dough and counter lightly with flour and turn dough out.
- Knead until dough is smooth and elastic, adding flour as necessary.
- Leave dough on counter, cover with a bowl, and rest 20~30 minutes.
- Preheat oven and baking stone or heavy inverted sheet pan to 475°F.
- Fold rested dough on itself a few times and divide in half.
- Return one half to covered bowl while you proceed with first half.
- Divide first half of dough into 4 equal size pieces, about 100 g each.
- Roll pieces (under the palm of your hand) to form smooth balls.
- Dust counter with flour; then flatten and roll first ball out to extremely thin.
- Bake on a very hot surface ~ 3 minutes until it puffs up and browns lightly.
- While the first piece bakes roll out the second ball.
- Flip (with pancake turner) and bake the other side 2~3 minutes.
- Remove from oven and carefully cut along edge to make 2 sheets.
- Rebake both sheets, raw side down, to brown lightly.
- Remove first batch from oven and continue baking remaining pieces.
- When first half of dough has been baked repeat steps with second half.

BREAD FAQS
frequently asked questions

My bread didn't rise as it should have. What did I do wrong?
A number of things can affect how bread rises. These are the most common:
- Old yeast - "proof" yeast in ¼ C of warm water with 2 TBS of flour and ¼ tsp of sugar
- Too cold - rise in a warm place ~ 95°F
- Not enough kneading to develop the gluten - knead longer
- Not enough time - some breads need hours to rise; be patient
- Flour with insufficient protein to create gluten - use better unbleached flour

My bread looked fine going in the oven but came out "squashed." What happened?
Your bread had probably risen past double in bulk when you put it into the oven. At this point, the gluten was stretched almost to its breaking point. When it entered the oven, the warmth caused what's called "oven spring" when the yeast grows like crazy before it is killed by the heat. Oven spring is normal, but it can push overly stretched gluten past its breaking point. To prevent this from happening, do not let your dough rise past double in bulk. If it has, knead it briefly and rise it again.

My bread tore open? What caused this?
Several things can cause bread to tear open, either during a rise or in the oven:
- Not enough kneading to develop the gluten - knead longer
- Flour with insufficient protein to create gluten - use better unbleached flour
- Rising too fast for the gluten's elasticity to keep up - rise cooler/slower

My bread was soggy inside. Why?
This is sometimes caused by cutting into bread hot from the oven before it has had a chance to cool sufficiently. When bread is taken from a hot oven, steam trapped inside by the crust continues to cook the crumb for several minutes as it cools. If you cut into hot bread, steam will be released and the cooking process will terminate prematurely. Soggy bread can also be caused by wrapping it in a moisture-proof barrier like plastic or foil before it has cooled completely to room temperature. To prevent soggy bread, allow it to cool to room temperature before cutting into it or wrapping it up. Of course, under-cooked bread will also be soggy, so be sure to bake it long enough. It is usually best to put bread back in the oven for 5 more minutes than risk taking it out before it is done.

Can I over-knead my dough?
It depends on how you are kneading. If you are kneading by hand, it would be nearly impossible to over-knead the dough. You'd likely pass out from exhaustion first! It is, however, more likely that you might add too much flour and end up with dry bread the longer you knead. If you are kneading by machine, either in a stand mixer or food processor, it is quite possible to over-knead. Food processors are extremely efficient, and the kneading process can be completed in seconds. Mixers take only a few minutes longer. Over-kneading can make bread tough.

Can I knead with my mixer using the dough hook?
It is very easy to over-flour when using a dough hook as you try to keep the dough from sticking to the bowl. For this reason, I recommend you use your mixer to combine the ingredients (using the paddle) and follow with kneading by hand. Experienced bakers known when they've added enough flour, but most new bakers don't. Learn what properly kneaded dough should look and feel like first.

How should I store my bread?
Bread should be stored either at room temperature or frozen. In either case, it should be sealed from oxygen in the air using heavy plastic or other barrier. Do not package bread until it has cooled to room temperature. If you wish to retire in the evening after baking and your bread is still warm, you can store it in the microwave (turned off!) overnight and package it in the morning.

BREAD FAQS
(continued)

Can I substitute whole wheat flour for white in my recipe?
Sometimes. If you are making an "authentic" or "classic" recipe, substituting whole wheat flour for what was specified will change the bread's taste and texture enough to distance the final product from the original. You would be wise to begin your introduction to whole wheat with a recipe designed for it. In so doing, the results will be somewhat more predictable as you gain experience with the new flour. Whole wheat often causes dough to be sticky compared to plain white flour, particularly those also containing molasses. For this reason, recipes containing whole wheat sometimes have added fat for improved handleability by less experienced bakers. If you do substitute whole wheat for white flour, start at 25% and work your way up 10% at a time with successive batches as you gain experience.

Can I substitute rye or oats for wheat flour?
Compared to wheat, rye and oats contain almost no gluten. For this reason, you should not simply substitute either for wheat when making bread. Instead, start with a recipe designed for the flours you are using. These often balance the flour's chemistry by including high-gluten bread flour or even by adding vital wheat gluten or both. Oat and rye breads usually include only one third non-wheat flours.

Can I substitute honey for sugar?
As far as sweetness is concerned, you can substitute honey for sugar (TBS for TBS). Bear in mind that using honey can make dough more sticky, and you will need good kneading skills to avoid adding too much flour. Keep the dough only lightly floured on the outside and yet slightly sticky on the inside during the kneading process. Be careful to avoid giving honey to children under age 2.

Can I substitute table salt for the "DC kosher" salt specified in your recipes?
Table salt is approximately twice as dense by volume as the Diamond Crystal kosher salt specified in these recipes. For this reason, if you need to use table salt cut the amount (by volume) in half. For recipes calling for 1 TBS of DC kosher salt, use 1½ tsp of table salt.

I'm on a low-salt diet. Can I reduce or eliminate the salt?
Bread with no salt tastes "flat." You can cut the salt by a third but I don't recommend going lower. This corresponds to using 2 tsp where 1 TBS is called for. Salt does two things in bread. It provides access to the full flavor of the grains. It also helps control the yeast from being too active, which can result in over-risen dough followed by dough that might collapse in the oven.

Why would you use oil or margarine instead of butter? Why both?
Members of my family and some of my students are lactose-intolerant. I often use canola oil or lactose-free margarine for this reason. Chefs often combine two fats in baking and cooking to realize the benefits of both. In breads, butter adds a nice flavor and other fats act as good tenderizers.

Can I use regular milk from the fridge instead of Instant Dry Milk specified?
Yes, with some caveats. There are enzymes in milk and a protein in the whey of milk that can interfere with dough rising to its full potential. To achieve maximum volume, deactivate these enzymes and protein by scalding milk to 180°F before using it to make yeast-risen breads. You may skip the scalding process, however, with only a slight loss of quality for doughs having a short rise cycle. Doughs with long rises retarded through refrigeration (e.g. rising overnight) may be particularly affected by milk that has not been scaled. Finally, using cold milk can slow yeast activity. If you are not scalding, warm milk to 95~100°F before using in a recipe with yeast.

How do I know when my bread is done?
Most breads will sound slightly hollow when tapped on the bottom if it is done. You can also use an instant-read thermometer to check the internal temperature which will be ~ 200°F when done.

TIPS FOR SAVING TIME
especially during colder months

Make dough in a stand mixer:
  Use the beater paddle (not the hook) to combine ingredients and mix the dough. The machine is very efficient and will accomplish this task much faster than you can by hand. Fortunately, using the machine will not detract from the quality of your finished product but may even enhance it by developing the gluten better than you might have by hand.

Use warm ingredients and equipment:
  Chances are your pantry or cupboard is cooler than your kitchen. If you plan on baking the next day, set out your flour container and mixing bowl on the counter the night before so they are at least at room temperature when you go to use them.

Rise in a warm oven:
  While rising too fast is not the goal, sometimes you need a little help, especially when making yeast breads in the winter. Turn on your oven for just a minute or two and bring it up to 100°F and then turn it off. An additional benefit of rising in the oven is that it prevents cold drafts from affecting your rising dough. Another technique is to place a pan of hot water in the bottom of the oven which will gently take the chill off the interior. Some high-end ovens even have a "proof cycle" built right into the controls that hold the oven at the proper temperature for rising yeast breads. Look for this feature the next time you shop for a new range or oven.

Rise on a heating pad:
  You can use this trick if your oven is already too hot from another task. Set the heating pad on the counter and turn it on to a low setting. Place your ceramic mixing bowl (covered with a layer of plastic wrap) on the pad and then drape a towel over the top to keep in the warmth. Check the temperature of the bowl; it should be just barely warm and not hot to the touch. If the bowl is too warm (over 100°F), put a towel under it so it is not directly on the heating pad.

Rise overnight:
  This is perhaps one of the best ways to save time on baking day. Get started the night before, and let the dough rise in the refrigerator overnight. This process is often used by artisan bakers to improve the complexity and flavors of their breads. A long gentle rise is generally preferred to a fast or forced rise. If using this tip with a dough containing milk, be sure to scald or use UHT (ultra-high temperature) milk for best results.

Try making dough in a food processor:
  Just understand that the food processor is so efficient, the mixing and kneading process is accomplished in a matter of seconds instead of minutes. You can over-knead using this trick, so start by reading the manual that came with your machine for guidance. There are also several books that focus on this technique; check your library. This is not recommended for light-duty or belt-driven machines; if the manual covers making dough you can give this a try. A food processor can actually generate enough friction that the dough is warmed during processing so pay attention to the recommended temperatures in the manual or book.

Choose a better recipe:
  When you find yourself in need of bread for a meal and are short on time, it is usually better to choose a bread designed for speed than to artificially force one into compliance. That's why this book contains recipes for corn bread, skillet bread, biscuits, and flatbreads.

ARTISAN BREAD TIPS
for advanced students

1. Use King Arthur flour. It is blended to be consistently high in the proteins that make up gluten. Their All-Purpose flour at 11.7% has almost as much protein as other brands' bread flours. Their Bread Flour is made from hard spring wheat and contains 12.7% protein, truly high-test flour. The main benefit of using KAF flours is their consistency bag-to-bag, season-to-season. Few flours, if any, come close. Once you perfect your bread making skills you can experiment with other flours, but until then this will eliminate one variable from the equation.

Note: Do NOT use bread flour for sweet breads, quick breads, biscuits, muffins, pancakes, scones, waffles, etc. or they will be tough! Use inexpensive, store brand, unbleached all-purpose flour for these products. Also, avoid bleached flours, even commercial / professional ones. Bleaching agents involve chemicals you simply don't need.

2. Use instant yeast as follows. Start with water at 120°F in your measuring cup. Pour it into your work bowl. Add an equal amount of flour by volume. Stir to make a batter. Check the temperature. If the batter is under 110°F stir in the instant yeast. If you have time, let it sit for 15~30 minutes "autolyse" while the sponge develops. Then mix in salt. Finally mix in a second equal amount of flour.

Here's how it works: Although you start with 120°~130°F water, the cold bowl will cool it a few degrees and the cold flour (from an unheated pantry or unheated cabinet) should cool it some more... hopefully to between 95~105°F. Letting it sit for a half hour gives the yeast a head-start on growing and developing flavors while the initial flour absorbs moisture. When you add the salt, the yeast growth may be cut in half, but at this point is should be growing like crazy. Adding the second dose of flour will drop the temperature further to just about right for the initial rise.

3. Use Diamond Crystal kosher salt. This is approximately half as dense as table salt. All recipes in this book are designed for it. If you substitute table salt cut the amount in half (by volume). This brand's crystals are essentially hollow and dissolve faster than other brands. It contains no iodine or free-flowing agents. It also doesn't seem to bounce as much when sprinkling on food.

Use the same salt all the time for consistency when making breads and other baked products. Sea salt, for example, varies in salinity depending on where it came from and how coarsely it was ground. Salt from the Dead Sea is different from Mediterranean sea salt which is different from Californian sea salt. As nice as sea salts are (and they are the rage these days), take the advice of Chef Michael Ruhlman and stick with one brand of kosher salt. As a bread topping, however, you can and should use coarse sea salt so the crystals won't dissolve.

4. Leave yourself reminders so you don't forget anything or add something twice. Measure yeast and salt out into ramekins on your work surface to remind you to add them. You've seen celebrity chefs on TV do this, and it's for a good reason.   (continued)

ARTISAN BREAD TIPS
(continued)

Later, if they're empty you'll know "it's in there." When you shape your dough and it is going through the final rise, leave your lame or serrated knife in front of the loaves as a reminder to slash them before they go into the oven. Similarly, put your spray bottle near the oven door as a reminder to spritz.

5. Don't over-flour. As soon as you go past 2x the volume of water by volume, be very careful to add as little flour as possible. For example, to make a small 2-loaf batch of demis, start with 2 C of water and be very careful once you go past 4 C of flour... using just enough on the outside to permit handling but keeping the inside as wet as possible.

For those of you with a digital scale, use the "bakers percentage" method and weight your ingredients. You want your water between 65~70%. Remember, bakers percentage is not of the total, but of the flour's weight. Artisan doughs often run as much as 75~80% hydration.

6. You can start your dough in a mixer, but finish it by hand. You can add twice as much flour as water by volume (see above) using the paddle on your mixer. After that, turn the dough out and finish it by hand, adding as little additional flour as possible.

7. Don't use a mixer's dough hook to knead. If you can use the hook without it sticking, you've already added too much flour. Dough hooks should be reserved for experts who know how to use them properly. You can mix with the machine, but knead by hand.

8. Never punch artisan dough down. You can stretch it out and fold it in thirds a couple of times after each rise. This is called "taking a turn on the dough." Treat risen artisan dough gently.

9. Take time. You can hurry things along using a little extra yeast and rising in a warm oven when absolutely necessary, like in class when we have only 2½ hours, but any other time you should slow things down. This will allow more flavor to develop. You can even use the refrigerator to retard the dough for an overnight rise.

10. Bake in a hot oven: 450°F would be a good place to start; you can bake artisan breads as high as 500°F. If you have a good convection oven you should bake 25~50 degrees lower.

11. Bake on a stone, like a #4467 by Old Stone Oven; it is 14x16" (rectangular) and cost around $40. A baking stone does several things for you. You don't even have to put the bread right on the stone to benefit. If you do your final rise on a sheet pan, you can place the pan on top of the stone. The heat from the stone will pass right through the pan into the bread. One of the main benefits from the thermal mass the stone adds to your oven is the ability to open the oven door several times for misting without loosing too much heat. Place the stone on the bottom of a gas oven or on a rack in the lowest position in an electric oven. Pre-heat the stone for a minimum of 45 minutes at temp or for an hour if starting with a cold stone in a cold oven.

Be careful lining your oven with products that are not food-grade. You don't want something in your oven that's out-gassing vapors from a heavy metal like lead or mercury!

ARTISAN BREAD TIPS
(continued)

12. Use semolina or flour to prevent sticking. Cornmeal burns at too low a temperature to be useful with artisan baking and should be avoided. Use semolina under dough whether you are baking on parchment, a baking sheet, in a cast iron skillet, or directly on the stone. Flour works, but some people don't like a coating on the bottom of their loaves and semolina is easier to brush off. You can usually find semolina in the pasta aisle at your market.

13. Always slash your bread just before it goes into the oven. This gives it a place to expand in the oven (called "oven spring") without cracking somewhere else where it would be less attractive. Use a sharp serrated knife for slashing if you don't have a "lame, " and do it with very fast strokes to prevent the knife from sticking to the dough and pulling it instead of cutting. Slashes don't need to be deep; a quarter inch is fine.

14. Spray your loaves with water several times: right before they go into the oven, and 1 or 2 more times at 2~3 minute intervals. This prevents a crust from forming and allows the "oven spring" to max out before the yeast is killed by the rising temperature in the dough. If you want to turn the pan to spray the far side be sure to do so gently until the dough has set.

I usually preheat a cast iron skillet on a rack near the top of the oven and boil water in a kettle on the stove just before baking. When the bread goes into the oven, the hot water goes into the skillet. This provides several minutes of intense steam and eliminates the need to open the door to spray. For even more and longer lasting steam, fill your skillet with clean lava rocks. You can get these at Walmart for about $4 for a 6# bag (enough to share with a couple of friends). Be VERY CAREFUL when performing this step, and wear long oven mitts.

Note: Trying to create steam in a standard gas oven is usually a waste of time. This is because gas ovens are vented as they need a supply of fresh air to support combustion.

15. Allow breads to cool before cutting into them. The cooking process does not end when breads come out of the oven. The steam trapped by the crust will continue cooking the crumb for some time, and if you cut into the hot dough the steam will escape and that cooking process will be terminated prematurely.

16. Once you've mastered the above, experiment with preferments. Simply mix water and flour in equal amounts by weight for a loose preferment called a "poolish." Mix in a very small amount of yeast, like a pinch or two. Let the poolish sit, covered, on the counter at room temperature for 6~8 hours to develop organic compounds which will improve your bread.

This technique was developed by Polish bakers who taught the French how to make bread ... not that they'd ever admit it! Italian bakers use a similar technique but start with a somewhat thicker preferment called a "biga." Besides consistency, the biga is usually allowed to ferment longer than a poolish, often overnight. You can also add a small amount of rye, perhaps 10% of the total flour in the recipe, when making rustic Italian bread to give it a little more flavor. Similarly, bakers often add some whole wheat flour to French breads or include a cup of sourdough starter which is sometimes as much as 50% whole wheat.

PRIMER ON PREFERMENTS
for advanced students

So, what is a preferment?

A preferment is quite simply some fermented dough. It includes a portion of the flour, water, and yeast (commercial or natural) in the recipe. Sometimes it also includes salt.

What are the benefits of a preferment?

Preferments can help improve artisan breads in a number of ways. First off, they add a significant layer of flavor that isn't typical of straight dough breads. This is because the preferment contains by-products of fermentation that take some time to develop. These by-products include acids and esters. You can taste these components as the "tang" in a sourdough, for example.

Preferments also improve the keeping quality of bread. This is partly due to the acidic nature of the resulting dough. The higher pH discourages the growth of bad microbes.

Preferments improve the dough's physical structure. The slightly increase in acidity helps strengthen the gluten that defines how strong the dough becomes and remains later on.

Preferments actually help shorten production time. While you could achieve a similar effect by retarding the dough, employing a preferment is a more efficient production method.

Finally, in certain flours, particularly rye types, there are a number of enzymes that can compromise the quality of bread by making the crumb gummy. The activity of these enzymes can be reduced by including a preferment that raises the dough's acidity slightly.

Are there other ways to achieve the same effect?

Yes, there are. You can slow the fermentation process down, a technique known as retarding, by either lowering the fermentation temperature, reducing the quantity of yeast, or both. While retarding certainly helps improve bread dough it is also somewhat inefficient, taking large amounts of time, and sometimes requiring refrigeration as well.

What are the different kinds of preferments and how to they differ?

pâte fermentée - perhaps the simplest form of preferment is nothing more than "old dough" that has been reserved from a previous batch of bread. This preferment alone contains salt.

poolish - a preferment developed by Polish bakers typically made from equal quantities of flour and water (by weight) with a very small amount of yeast added to start fermentation.

biga - an Italian-style preferment, typically somewhat stiffer in consistency when compared to a poolish. The advantage of a biga is that the stiffer it is, the longer it can be allowed to ferment without becoming "over-ripe"; biga is, therefore, less time-sensitive than poolish.

sourdough - often called levain or starter, is made using natural instead of commercial yeast. It is somewhat more fragile, needs to be "fed" prior to use, and can take significant time to work its magic, both flavoring and leavening the bread. You can, however, use sourdough or levain as a flavoring for breads leavened with commercial yeast. Some sourdough starters include rye or whole wheat as well as white flour.

PRIMER ON PREFERMENTS
(continued)

So, how do I use a preferment?
  The preferment is made hours or sometimes a day in advance of making the dough. In all cases, some advance planning is required. You can't start a recipe requiring a preferment at noon and expect to have finished bread for dinner. Similarly, you shouldn't start an extended process today you don't have adequate time to complete tomorrow.

  Start by mixing a simple poolish style preferment:
  1. For a typical 2-loaf bread recipe, measure 1 cup of room temperature water into a bowl.
  2. Add an equal weight of flour or approximately twice as much by volume, ~ 2 cups.
  3. Stir to form a batter, and then mix in a small amount of yeast: ¼ teaspoon or ¾ gram.
  4. Cover loosely to let the fermentation gases escape.
  5. Allow the batter to ferment at room temperature 6~8 hours or until triple in bulk
  6. Add the preferment to your bread dough, typically at the batter stage.

Why do the recipes in this book with preferments often include very hot water?
  When you add a cup or more of preferment (at room temperature) to the normal bread-making process, the temperature of the dough will drop significantly. This is not really a huge problem at home where you can let your dough rise as long as required to double in bulk. In bread class, however, we have a very limited amount of time to make dough and bake it off. That said, the recipes in this book are highly optimized for speed to allow the entire process to be completed in the allotted 2½ hours of a typical bread class.

  When we add hot water, sometimes as hot as 200°F, to the preferment the resulting temperature should be between 110°F ~ 120°F. In the next step we typically add another cup or two of flour, which drops the temperature of the batter to around 100°F, just right to add our yeast and proceed with autolyse and bulk fermentation. This is no accident, but a carefully planned and tested process that works well and is highly repeatable.

How should I modify the recipes in this book when baking at home?
  Generally, you won't be in as much of a hurry as we are in class. If this is indeed the case, you can slow the whole process down, and you will actually be rewarded for doing so with superior products that will likely taste better and have better structure (crust and crumb).

  That said, when a recipe specifies adding very hot water to the preferment, you could simply substitute warm water at 110°F ~ 120°F. This will do a number of things besides slow the fermentation process down. The very hot water we use in class actually sacrifices the yeast in the preferment. While we gain significant flavor from the preferment, we don't see much benefit from it as a leavening agent; we rely entirely on the yeast added later on.

What are the relationships between preferment ingredients, temperature, time, and results?
  Adding flour to the preferment (i.e. biga vs. poolish) increases fermentation time.
  Adding flour to the preferment also reduces the flour needed later on in the recipe.
  Adding yeast to the preferment decreases fermentation time.
  A warmer temperature (of ingredients or in the room) decreases fermentation time.
  Longer fermentation generally yields more acidity and adds more flavor to your bread.
  Increasing the amount of preferment (%) in a recipe adds complexity and flavor as well.

DOUGH SCORING DESIGNS
for Boules & Baguettes

DOUGH SCORING DESIGNS
for Batards

Single Line

Triple French Cut

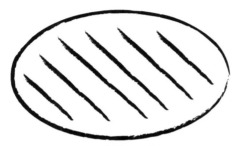
Diagonal Saucisson

Diamond Crosshatch

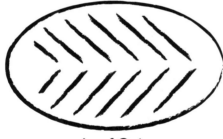
Leaf Cut

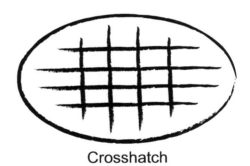
Crosshatch

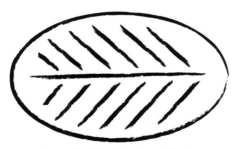
Leaf with Center Cut

"S" Cut

WEIGHTS OF BAKING INGREDIENTS
in grams

	1 C	¾ C	⅔ C	½ C	⅓ C	¼ C	TBS	tsp
Baking Powder/Soda	221	166	147	111	74	55	13.8	4.6
Butter	226	170	151	113	75	57	14.1	4.7
Chocolate Chips	170	128	113	85	57	43	10.6	3.5
Cocoa Powder	86	65	57	43	29	22	5.4	1.8
Coconut, shredded	71	53	47	36	24	18	4.4	1.5
Corn Syrup, dark	328	246	219	164	109	82	20.5	6.8
Corn Syrup, light	341	256	227	171	114	85	21.3	7.1
Cornmeal, coarse	130	98	87	65	43	33	8.1	2.7
Cream, heavy/sour	232	174	155	116	77	58	14.5	4.8
Flour, all-purpose	120	90	80	60	40	30	7.5	2.5
Honey	340	255	227	170	113	85	21.3	7.1
Lard	205	154	137	103	68	51	12.8	4.3
Maple Syrup	315	236	210	158	105	79	19.7	6.6
Milk, instant dry	69	52	46	35	23	17	4.3	1.4
Milk, whole	244	183	163	122	81	61	15.3	5.1
Molasses	337	253	225	169	112	84	21.1	7.0
Oats, flour	104	78	69	52	35	26	6.5	2.2
Oats, rolled	80	60	53	40	27	20	5.0	1.7
Oil, vegetable	224	168	149	112	75	56	14.0	4.7
Potato, instant flakes	66	50	44	33	22	17	4.1	1.4
Raisins, packed	160	120	107	80	53	40	10.0	3.3
Raisins, unpacked	144	108	96	72	48	36	9.0	3.0
Salt, DC kosher	160	120	107	80	53	40	10.0	3.3
Salt, table	314	236	209	157	105	79	19.6	6.5
Semolina	168	126	112	84	56	42	10.5	3.5
Shortening, vegetable	205	154	137	103	68	51	12.8	4.3
Sugar, confectioners	115	86	77	58	38	29	7.2	2.4
Sugar, dark brown packed	238	179	159	119	79	60	14.9	5.0
Sugar, granulated	200	150	133	100	67	50	12.5	4.2
Sugar, light brown packed	218	164	145	109	73	55	13.6	4.5
Vanilla Extract	208	156	139	104	69	52	13.0	4.3
Water	236	177	157	118	79	59	14.8	4.9
Yeast, instant	150	113	100	75	50	38	9.4	3.1
Yogurt	245	184	163	123	82	61	15.3	5.1
Large Egg no shell	50	each						
Large Egg Yolk	19	each						
Large Egg White	30	each						

WEIGHTS OF BAKING INGREDIENTS
in ounces

	1 C	¾ C	⅔ C	½ C	⅓ C	¼ C	TBS	tsp
Baking Powder/Soda	7.8	5.8	5.2	3.9	2.6	1.9	0.5	0.2
Butter	8.0	6.0	5.3	4.0	2.7	2.0	0.5	0.2
Chocolate Chips	6.0	4.5	4.0	3.0	2.0	1.5	0.4	0.1
Cocoa Powder	3.0	2.3	2.0	1.5	1.0	0.8	0.2	0.1
Coconut, shredded	2.5	1.9	1.7	1.3	0.8	0.6	0.2	0.1
Corn Syrup, dark	11.6	8.7	7.7	5.8	3.9	2.9	0.7	0.2
Corn Syrup, light	12.0	9.0	8.0	6.0	4.0	3.0	0.8	0.3
Cornmeal, coarse	4.6	3.4	3.1	2.3	1.5	1.1	0.3	0.1
Cream, heavy/sour	8.2	6.1	5.5	4.1	2.7	2.0	0.5	0.2
Flour, all-purpose	4.2	3.2	2.8	2.1	1.4	1.1	0.3	0.1
Honey	12.0	9.0	8.0	6.0	4.0	3.0	0.7	0.2
Lard	7.2	5.4	4.8	3.6	2.4	1.8	0.5	0.2
Maple Syrup	11.1	8.3	7.4	5.6	3.7	2.8	0.7	0.2
Milk, instant dry	2.4	1.8	1.6	1.2	0.8	0.6	0.2	0.1
Milk, whole	8.6	6.5	5.7	4.3	2.9	2.2	0.5	0.2
Molasses	11.9	8.9	7.9	5.9	4.0	3.0	0.7	0.2
Oats, flour	3.7	2.8	2.4	1.8	1.2	0.9	0.2	0.1
Oats, rolled	2.8	2.1	1.9	1.4	0.9	0.7	0.2	0.1
Oil, vegetable	7.9	5.9	5.3	4.0	2.6	2.0	0.5	0.2
Potato, instant flakes	2.3	1.7	1.6	1.2	0.8	0.6	0.1	0.0
Raisins, packed	5.6	4.2	3.8	2.8	1.9	1.4	0.4	0.1
Raisins, unpacked	5.1	3.8	3.4	2.5	1.7	1.3	0.3	0.1
Salt, DC kosher	5.6	4.2	3.8	2.8	1.9	1.4	0.4	0.1
Salt, table	11.1	8.3	7.4	5.5	3.7	2.8	0.7	0.2
Semolina	5.9	4.4	4.0	3.0	2.0	1.5	0.4	0.1
Shortening, vegetable	7.2	5.4	4.8	3.6	2.4	1.8	0.5	0.2
Sugar, confectioners	4.1	3.0	2.7	2.0	1.4	1.0	0.3	0.1
Sugar, dark brown packed	8.4	6.3	5.6	4.2	2.8	2.1	0.5	0.2
Sugar, granulated	7.1	5.3	4.7	3.5	2.4	1.8	0.4	0.1
Sugar, light brown packed	7.7	5.8	5.1	3.8	2.6	1.9	0.5	0.2
Vanilla Extract	7.3	5.5	4.9	3.7	2.4	1.8	0.5	0.2
Water	8.3	6.2	5.5	4.2	2.8	2.1	0.5	0.2
Yeast, instant	5.3	4.0	3.5	2.6	1.8	1.3	0.3	0.1
Yogurt	8.6	6.5	5.8	4.3	2.9	2.2	0.5	0.2
Large Egg no shell	1.8	each						
Large Egg Yolk	0.7	each						
Large Egg White	1.1	each						

TEMPERATURE CONVERSIONS
Fahrenheit to Celsius

70°F	21°C	Room Temperature
100°F	38°C	Body Temperature
125°F	52°C	Warm Water
140°F	60°C	Scalding Hot Water
180°F	82°C	Scalded Milk
200°F	93°C	Almost Boiling
212°F	100°C	Water Boils
225°F	107°C	Very Cool Oven
250°F	121°C	Very Slow Oven
275°F	135°C	Very Slow Oven
300°F	149°C	Slow Oven
325°F	163°C	Slow Oven
350°F	177°C	Moderate Oven
375°F	191°C	Moderate Oven
400°F	204°C	Moderately Hot Oven
425°F	218°C	Hot Oven
450°F	232°C	Hot Oven
475°F	246°C	Hot Oven
500°F	260°C	Extremely Hot Oven
525°F	274°C	Extremely Hot Oven
550°F	288°C	Broiling Oven

Made in the USA
San Bernardino,
CA